CONCORD
AND THE
CIVIL WAR

From Walden Pond to the Gettysburg Front

RICK FRESE

Charleston · London

THE
History
PRESS

Published by The History Press
Charleston, SC 29403
www.historypress.net

Copyright © 2014 by Rick Frese
All rights reserved

First published 2014

Manufactured in the United States

ISBN 978.1.62619.294.2

Library of Congress CIP data applied for.

To my wife, Nancy James, whose love and encouragement is appreciated every single day!

CONTENTS

Acknowledgements

I begin with a special thanks to my now thirteen-year-old buddy, Michael Carr, who walked sacred ground with me at the site of the Battles of Bull Run in Manassas, Virginia. My great-grandfather Frederick Frese enlisted in the Union army shortly after the firing at Fort Sumter and was with the 8th New York Infantry at First and Second Bull Run. He was a wagon master and company bugler. That bugle has passed from father to son over four generations. In 2011, I was honored to accompany Michael and his Landon School classmates on another memorable tour, traveling from Bethesda, Maryland, to the Gettysburg Battlefield.

I am especially grateful to Tom Smith, my friend and teammate in the Concord Baseball Club, who read the manuscript and made it better. I received much-appreciated help from Archivist Leslie Wilson and her assistant, Conni Manoli-Skocay, at the Concord Free Public Library. Tish Hopkins, Concord Cemetery supervisor, kindly provided permission to take photographs of some Civil War veterans' graves in Sleepy Hollow.

It's been my good fortune over the course of four decades to have worked with a cadre of supportive department chairs at Bentley University; so, I extend my gratitude to Gary David, Angela Garcia, Tim Anderson, Shiping Zheng, Greg Hall, Christine Williams, the late Stewart Shapiro, Tony Kimball and Herb Sawyer, who paved the way. Thanks, too, are due academic administrative assistants Darlene Saunders, Doreen McBride and Janice McMahon. My indebtedness to these colleagues, along with administrators and academic deans, is genuine and profound.

ACKNOWLEDGEMENTS

A special thanks to the brilliant writer and historian Doris Kearns Goodwin, her son Joe and daughter-in-law Victoria for recognizing that the Civil War was a largely untreated chapter in our town's history and, as such, cheering me on in this project. Additionally, the Concord Museum's 2011 exhibit When Duty Whispers: Concord and the Civil War sparked renewed interest in researching Concord in the 1860s.

A book project is a collaboration, and so I truly appreciate the ongoing guidance provided by Katie Orlando, my commissioning editor at The History Press. She has been a real asset.

I pay tribute to my mother, Mary Rushe (Frese), who grew up across from Sleepy Hollow Cemetery in Concord, and to her highly decorated brother, Barney Rushe, who was among the first to storm Omaha Beach on D-Day with the Fighting First Division, the "Big Red One."

Without the steadfast encouragement and loving support of my wife, Nancy James-Frese, this project might not have been undertaken. Thank you, Nancy, for urging me to write this book, which is dedicated to you.

Lastly, I salute marine First Lieutenant Derek Brozowski, who, following a tradition established by the Concord Artillery, has served his town and nation with pride and distinction.

INTRODUCTION

On the morning of Monday, April 15, 1861, headlines screamed that "highly important news" was emerging from Washington. President Lincoln had just issued a proclamation to call forth seventy-five thousand militia troops to suppress Southern military action, as recruiting posters declared, "VOLUNTEERS WANTED." The threat of a Confederate attack against the nation's capital had not been anticipated, but it now seemed terribly imminent. Three days later, a young, newly minted soldier from Concord, Massachusetts, explained his decision to join the 6th Massachusetts Regiment: "When the order came for me to join my unit, sir, I was plowing in the same field at Concord where my grandfather was plowing when the British fired on the Massachusetts men at Lexington. He did not wait a moment and I did not, sir." Responding to the emergency proclamation, many a Concord farmer would "leave the plow in furrow."[1]

Exactly four years later, the selectmen of Concord would issue their own broadside, "requesting that all labor and business be suspended on April 19th, between the hours of 11 and 2 o'clock." For on that day, Concord would "unite in the solemnities to be observed by the whole country at the hour of the funeral of Abraham Lincoln, the Late President of the United States."

From 1861 to 1865, the names of more than 450 men appeared on the Concord muster rolls, men who fought in the U.S. Army or Navy "for cause and comrades."[2] On April 19, 1867, a thirty-foot-high obelisk was dedicated in the center of town in memory of Concord's Civil War veterans, forty-

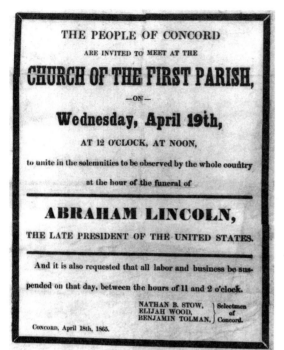

THE PEOPLE OF CONCORD

ARE INVITED TO MEET AT THE

CHURCH OF THE FIRST PARISH,

—ON—

Wednesday, April 19th,

AT 12 O'CLOCK, AT NOON,

to unite in the solemnities to be observed by the whole country

at the hour of the funeral of

ABRAHAM LINCOLN,

THE LATE PRESIDENT OF THE UNITED STATES.

And it is also requested that all labor and business be suspended on that day, between the hours of 11 and 2 o'clock.

NATHAN B. STOW, } Selectmen
ELIJAH WOOD, of
BENJAMIN TOLMAN, } Concord.

CONCORD, April 18th, 1865.

Left: Lincoln's memorial service in Concord, April 19, 1865. *Author's collection.*

Below: Concord's Civil War monument circa 1900. *Author's collection.*

eight of whom had made the supreme sacrifice. Inscribed on the monument are these words: "The Town of Concord builds this monument in honor of the brave men whose names it bears and records with grateful pride that they found here a birthplace home or grave" ["Faithful Unto Death"].

Calling attention to a citizen's highest calling, Ralph Waldo Emerson, the "Voice of Concord," affirmed, while all were listening to the cannon salute, that "though the cannon volleys have the sound of funeral echoes, they can yet hear through [these echoes] the benedictions of their country." Prominent Concord names were among these honored dead: Lieutenant Ezra Ripley, Colonel George Prescott, Francis Buttrick, William Damon and, most tragically, the three Melvin brothers—Asa, John and Samuel. At the annual town meeting held on April 1, 1907, a committee of seven was appointed and charged with the task of recording the names of the men who served. Since no official records were kept in Concord during the Civil War, the committee researched reports of the adjutant-general of Massachusetts, as well as recollections of veterans and older citizens. Ultimately, they identified more than 450 veterans of the conflict, 122 of whom (by 1908) were interred in Concord cemeteries.

The prototypical Northern soldier in the War of the Rebellion, as it was called, was under thirty, lacking in property and perhaps an Irish or German immigrant, since they made up almost one-third of the Federal volunteer forces. Enlistments varied along socioeconomic lines, and the ranks were filled with clerks, farm laborers and skilled workers, many of whom were motivated by the lure of bounties and pay as a means of moving out of privation. Regardless of the attraction, these were Northern men who possessed an earnest sense of duty. Their letters are replete with statements of "sacrificing my personal feelings and inclination…My duty in the hour of danger"—a willingness to "give up my life if need be."[3] The first Union officer to fall, shot and killed on May 24, 1861, wore a gold medal on his chest with the words *Non nobis, sed pro patria* inscribed, meaning, "Not for ourselves, but for country." Our Concord soldiers fell on the battlefields at Antietam, Vicksburg, Bull Run, Gettysburg, Petersburg and Port Hudson, Louisiana. Witness to this "War of the Attempted Secession," the poet Walt Whitman lamented "the dead, the dead, the dead, our dead—South or North—ours all…our young men, once so handsome and joyous, taken from us—the son from the mother, the husband from the wife, the dear friend from the dear friend…[oh these] clusters of many graves."

For some time, the total number of Civil War dead was thought to be 620,000. (The population of the United States in 1860 was 31.5 million.)

Recent research suggests that the actual number may have exceeded 700,000. Using this figure, if the same percentage of Americans were to be killed in war today, the number of American dead might be more than 7 million. The scale of this conflict, what our sixteenth president called "this mighty scourge of war," produced what contemporaries referred to as "a harvest of death," resulting in horrific cost in blood and treasure.

While the largest percentage of battlefield deaths and injuries was caused by rifle bullets (Minié balls predominately), twice as many Civil War soldiers died from diseases. In total, more than 400,000 combatants on both sides became POWs, and more than 55,000 of them died during incarceration. Of the 45,000 Union prisoners held at Georgia's Andersonville Prison (aka Camp Sumter), 12,913 died due to starvation, malnutrition, malarial fever, typhoid, consumption, diarrhea and other diseases. One prisoner, upon entering this camp, described men as "nothing more than mere walking skeletons, covered with filth and vermin…can this be hell?" Concord's Samuel Melvin, brother of two fallen soldiers, was taken prisoner near Spotsylvania, Virginia, and delivered to Andersonville, where he died of a lingering sickness in September 1864. The 1882 Concord Town Report reveals that his daily prison diary exhibited a "record of inhumanity and torture that is hardly equaled by anything that has been published concerning any of the rebel prisons." These horrors were in evidence in the stockade in Salisbury, North Carolina, which held 11,000 prisoners in late 1864—roughly 8,500 of them died while incarcerated. The daily average for morning burials was forty, but sixty was not uncommon. With very few tents on the compound, significant numbers of men lived in holes in the ground. Some froze to death, while others suffered from frozen limbs. The food staple was a meal of corn in which the cob and husk were ground together. All the most wretched conditions imaginable were there.

The soldiers of Concord went to war fully comprehending the political issues involved in the split between North and South. On the occasion of Concord's 250th anniversary celebration in 1885, the Honorable George F. Hoar spoke of "the men who have come out from our farm-houses…ready for the great self-sacrifices of life…country, honor and duty had meaning for them." This book salutes *our* Concord soldiers for the manner in which they affirmed love for their country, and we should also pay tribute to all those on the homefront who made their own sacrifices.

Chapter 1

THE ANTEBELLUM PERIOD AND THE RISE OF THE ANTISLAVERY MOVEMENT IN CONCORD, 1830–1860

In *To Set This World Right*, Sandra H. Petrulionis suggested that Concord may have been the most significant intellectual center in antebellum America. Clearly, this town occupied a very special place where abolitionist views were spawned by activists amid a culture in which reform movements flourished. Beginning in the 1830s, we see the first stirrings of strong resistance to the "sin of slavery" and the emergence of Concord connections to prominent antislavery leaders in Boston. Framing antislavery ideology during this period, we can trace the evolution of abolitionist sentiment in Concord:

January 1, 1831: William Lloyd Garrison publishes the first edition of the *Liberator*, which becomes the most significant antislavery newspaper in the nation.

1832: Garrison and eleven other men create the New England Anti-Slavery Society.

1834: The Middlesex County Anti-Slavery Society is formed in Groton, Massachusetts.

1836: The Transcendental Club begins in Boston and Concord, with prominent intellectuals, clergymen and reformers in the ranks. (Ralph Waldo Emerson, who moved to Concord the year before, is its most notable member.)

1837: The Concord Female Anti-Slavery Society is founded. Dozens of Concord women will hold fundraisers to fuel Garrison's abolitionist activities.

1838: Concord women file two antislavery petitions to the U.S. Congress. These petitions advocate an end to the slave trade, the abolition of slavery in the nation's capitol and resistance to the annexation of Texas.

1842: Abolitionist Wendell Phillips, speaking on "Slavery," addresses an audience at the Concord Lyceum.

1845: Frederick Douglass, an escaped slave, orator and abolitionist, publishes his *Narrative*. Douglass first appears in Concord in 1841, when he speaks at the new Universalist meetinghouse. (That church in Monument Square transitioned to St. Bernard's in 1863.)

1848: Abolitionist activists Lucretia Mott and Elizabeth Cady Stanton, Bronson Alcott's friend, convene the Seneca Falls Convention on women's rights. Women's enfranchisement will become an extension of the antislavery movement.

1850: The Fugitive Slave Act takes effect. Antislavery speeches become more volatile. Mary Moody Emerson and Lidian Emerson, Waldo's wife, attempt to ignite passions in Concord for this violation of "the Law of God." Concord abolitionists become more actively connected to the Vigilance Committee, a Boston-based group aiding fugitive slaves in the area.

1851: Concord's antislavery efforts intensify with direct links established with the "Underground Railroad," assisting fugitive men and women of color.

1852: Harriet Beecher Stowe publishes *Uncle Tom's Cabin*; initially a series of articles in abolitionist newspapers, this becomes a national bestseller. Stowe and Emerson were distant cousins, and both were offspring of notable Boston ministers.

1854: On January 25, William Whiting—Concord harness maker and activist in the abolitionist cause and now vice-president of the state's antislavery society—attends the annual convocation in Boston. President Franklin Pierce, denounced as a servile tool of slavery leaders, is called "the vilest of all tyrants." In late June, Waldo Emerson and a host of Concord abolitionists gather to resolve "That the Fugitive Slave Law must be repealed." In mid-July, Theodore Parker delivers his fiery speech in Concord, proclaiming that "the darkest periods of the American Revolution" did not compare with the current crisis…our enemy is no longer a foreign power…now our enemy is at home."

1855: William Lloyd Garrison and Wendell Phillips are in attendance at the Middlesex County Anti-Slavery Society meeting held in Concord on June 29. On July 4, Mrs. R.W. Emerson drapes her front gate in black in condemnation of the Fugitive Slave Act.

1856: John Brown, accompanied by a party of several men, including his four sons, engage in the Pottawatomie Creek massacre, killing five proslavery Kansans, in retaliation for five Free-Soil settlers killed earlier. Brown is now a wanted fugitive. Two days after the Pottawatomie slaughter, viewing a deepening split between North and South, Emerson appears at an "Indignation meeting in Concord" and states, "I do not see how a barbarous community and a civilized community can constitute one state. I think we must get rid of slavery, or we must get rid of freedom."[4]

1857: Franklin Sanborn, Concord schoolmaster and a member of the "Secret Six" raising money for John Brown, delivers an invitation to Brown to speak at a gathering sponsored by the Concord Female Anti-Slavery Society. On March 11, Brown addresses a crowd of one hundred people at the Concord Town House. Emerson and Thoreau are in the audience. After hearing Brown speak about his "Cause for Freedom" and the situation dividing pro- and antislavery settlers in Kansas, Emerson donates twenty-five dollars, with Thoreau contributing "a trifle." Truly impressed with Brown, Daniel Foster, former minister of Concord's Trinitarian Church, decides to become a crusader for Brown's cause, traveling to Kansas to serve in Captain Brown's company and participate in the next Kansas bloody engagement.

1858: Louisa May Alcott and her three sisters organize the "Dramatic Union" (forerunner to the Concord Players, still thriving today). They put their theatrical talents to work staging skits to raise money for the Concord Female Anti-Slavery Society. Franklin Sanborn participates, creating a staged slavery piece.

1859: *A Midsummer Night's Dream* is staged as a fundraiser for the Female Anti-Slavery Society by L.M. Alcott. John Brown returns to Concord in May, spending three days as Sanborn's guest at his Sudbury Road home. Seeking financial aid and guns, he again

Louisa May Alcott, seated, reading. *Conly's Portraits, Concord Free Public Library.*

Grand Review, Concord, Massachusetts, from *Harper's Weekly*, 1859. *Author's collection.*

speaks at the Town House, with Emerson, Thoreau and Bronson Alcott in attendance. This time, he raises $2,000 from townspeople. Five months later, he and a band of twenty-one men attack Harper's Ferry. The raid ends when U.S. marines under the command of Lieutenant Colonel

Robert E. Lee kill ten of Brown's men. Brown is found guilty of treason and hanged on December 2. While many view him as a fanatic, he is seen by others as a martyred saint. On the day of his execution, there is a memorial service at First Church in Concord, organized by Thoreau. Delivering his eulogy, Reverend Edmund Sears, author of the Christmas carol "It Came Upon a Midnight Clear," reads this poem: "Not any spot six feet by two—Will hold a man like thee—John Brown will tramp the shaking earth—From Blue Ridge to the sea." Apparently, this was the inspiration for the Union army's marching song "John Brown's Body." While Thoreau, Sanborn and Alcott pay tribute to Brown, others hang and burn Brown in effigy on the lawn outside the Lexington Road church.

On April 3, 1859, U.S. marshals forcibly removed Franklin Sanborn from his 5 Sudbury Road home to place him under arrest for his complicity in the Harper's Ferry raid launched by Brown. Ebenezer Hoar, justice of the Massachusetts Supreme Judicial Court, issued a writ of habeus corpus from his home, a block away from Sanborn's, thus preventing the arrest.

From September 7–9, 1859, Camp Massachusetts was held in Concord. This general muster consisted of six thousand troops under the command of Governor and General Nathaniel Banks. Gathering on the parade grounds of what is now the state prison, this encampment attracted tens of thousands of spectators (estimates of the crowd range from 50,000 to 100,000). Writing in *Concord in War Times*, Reverend Grindall Reynolds, minister of Concord's First Parish Church, described the scene as follows: "Concord has rarely been more thoroughly alive than when these thousands tramped, in what seemed an interminable procession, from the muster field through our dusty streets to the site of the old North Bridge." This was the first time any state had mobilized all militia units at one time. It now seemed terribly clear that something was about to happen.

Chapter 2

CONCORD AND THE ROAD TO WAR

The population of the town of Concord in the 1830s was about 2,000, with just 36 people of color, but like the country itself, this comfortable town was moving beyond its Revolutionary past into a new age. It was a time of significant change, with technological, industrial and economic advances in manufacturing and trade. Improved transportation systems expanded Concord's connections to Boston and well beyond, and by 1832, there were 106 stagecoach lines in Boston, with the Boston–Groton stage route making forty trips a week, with stops at Concord's inn, bringing 350 people into town each week. (With stage stops, the eighteen-mile trip from Boston to Concord took three to four hours.) In 1830, the Boston & Lowell Railroad was chartered, with the Fitchburg connection through Concord operational in 1843.

Communication lines made a dramatic breakthrough in 1838 when Samuel Morse demonstrated the telegraph, and in 1844, the first telegraph link was established between Washington and Baltimore. A Western Union telegraph was formed in 1856, and by 1860, telegraph lines had blanketed the American landscape. (Actually, Harrison Gray Dyar of Concord preempted Morse by stringing the first telegraph line along the "Causeway," now Lowell Road, over the Concord River at Hunt's Bridge.)

The first postal mailboxes appeared in Boston and New York City in 1858. Daily newspapers arrived in the early 1830s, and within twenty years, Boston newspaper boys posted at the train station were hawking copies of the *Daily Advertiser, Boston Evening Transcript, Boston Post, Boston Herald, Boston*

Traveler, *Daily Bee*, *Daily Journal*, *Morning Journal* and the *Gazette*. This resulted in a huge readership, with people ravenous for news of the day, and Concord was no exception, as readers stayed informed of abolitionist activities from the print media.

Beyond antislavery organizations, Boston was fertile ground for a multitude of organizations devoted to "do-good" causes. These organizations included the Boston Society for the Prevention of Pauperism, the Boston Society for Propagating the Gospel among the Indians, the Boston Infidel Relief Society, the Boston Temperance Association, the Boston Female Moral Reform Society and the Boston Total Abstinence Society, among others. No wonder Bronson Alcott described Boston as "a city in our world, upon which the light of the sun of righteousness has risen…the source whence every stream of thought and purpose emanates."[5]

With Boston as something of a Holy See of the abolitionist movement, this city on the hill truly enjoyed a philosophical, intellectual and activist connection to Concord. The Emersons, Alcotts, Thoreau and Sanborn formed a familial bond with Garrison, Phillips, Elizabeth Cady Stanton, H.B. Stowe, Frederick Douglass and John Brown. One current Concord historian referred to these relationships as "three degrees of separation"— the idea that everyone and everything is three or fewer steps away from one another, and thus any two people can be connected in a maximum of three steps. We will see these connections play out in other ways in mideighteenth-century America.

In September 1848, Congressman Abraham Lincoln began an eleven-day trip to Massachusetts that was to be the future president's only stay in Boston. As a delegate to the 1848 Whig national convention in Philadelphia, he supported the candidacy of Zachary Taylor and campaigned for him. Referring to himself as being "from the wild west and with hayseed in my hair," Lincoln traveled to "the most cultured state in the Union," where, no doubt, Concord Whig Party members were in attendance at his Boston appearances. William Stevens Robinson, for a brief period the editor of the *Yeoman's Gazette*, the Concord Whig organ, supported the Whig cause as the best hope for eliminating slavery. Mary M. Brooks, the wife of Nathan Brooks, a prominent local Whig, headed the Ladies Anti-Slavery Society in Concord.

Lincoln spoke first at the Boston Whig Club at 21 Bromfield Street, a "ladder street" between Tremont and Washington in Boston, and also at 36 Bromfield, where John Wilkes Booth had once boarded. He spoke again the next day at Lorimer Hall at the Tremont Temple Church; this was a former theater that had been managed by Junius Brutus Booth, famed tragedian and father of John Wilkes. The keynote speaker at this event, whom Lincoln met for the first time, was Lincoln's future secretary of state and former New York governor William Seward. In April 1865, Seward would also be attacked in Booth's assassination conspiracy.

Pursuing this circular pattern of relationships a bit further, Julia Ward Howe, author of the "Battle Hymn of the Republic" and abolitionist friend of both Emerson and Sanborn, had been infatuated with Edwin Booth, Wilkes's brother and a prominent actor in his own right. In 1854, Edwin fell in love with Laura Keene, who was on the stage at Ford's Theater the night Lincoln was shot and immediately rushed to comfort the fallen president. In 1863 or 1864, Edwin Booth saved Lincoln's son's life. Robert Todd Lincoln, on break from Harvard and standing in line at a train station in Jersey City, was pushed by the crowd against the train. When the train began to move, he fell into the gap between the train and the platform; suddenly, hands grabbed his coat collar and pulled him to safety. He turned and recognized Edwin Booth as his rescuer. Accompanying Booth on this trip was John T. Ford, owner of Washington's Ford's Theater. Edwin Booth, wife Mary Devlin Booth and Julia Ward Howe are all interred at famed Mount Auburn Cemetery in Cambridge. For more than a century, it was widely believed that Robert Lincoln had a romantic relationship with Lucy Hale, daughter of a New Hampshire senator and future fiancée of John Wilkes Booth. So, we witness a complex web of relationships among prominent Washington, Boston and Concord contemporaries at a most fateful time in American history—the ascension of Lincoln to the presidency and the Civil War that followed.

In 1860, Concord's population grew to 2,246, with town records listing 14 free colored persons. While very much a renowned nineteenth-century literary center, it still maintained a village character, with farming and trade being principal economic activities. There were sixteen marriages recorded during the year and sixteen interments reported by the cemetery committee, with the average length of life tabulated as thirty-three and three-fourths years. The leading causes of death included cholera, apoplexy and consumption; other causes included typhoid fever, diarrhea, dysentery, scarlet fever, measles and just one from "old age." There were 3,105 books in the town library, with total library expenses being $287.00; $5.23 was collected in fines. The fire department budget included a line item identifying an expenditure of $0.35 for a sponge and towel. In his annual report, the superintendent of public grounds described, in some detail, the destruction of trees in front of Cyrus Stow's home. They were broken down and destroyed by "some rowdy, good for nothing youths…in a spirit of vandalism…they were no better than savages."

In 1861, Bronson Alcott, superintendent of schools, submitted a sixty-eight-page report to the selectmen describing the previous school year and highlighting the regulations mandating that schools open at 9:00 a.m. by reading the scriptures, followed by the Lord's Prayer. If "a *scholar* be absent, it requires a written excuse from the parent or guardian." All candidates for high school were required to pass exams in reading, spelling, grammar, arithmetic, geography and the history of the United States. The town appropriated $3,300 for all schools, including acquisition of these high school books: *Arnold's Latin and Greek Series*; works by Virgil, Milton and Shakespeare; Homer's *Iliad*; books on French grammar; and *Plutarch's Lives*. Students were expected to complete course work in algebra, geometry, philosophy, astronomy, chemistry, geology, botany and U.S. history. Alcott proposed compiling a Concord book from the writings of townsmen and women that would include selections from town founder Peter Bulkeley, Ripley, Hoar, Hawthorne, Channing, Thoreau and Emerson. All of this was consistent with Alcott's master plan to "refine the mind, manners and morals" of Concord's young people.

As superintendent, Alcott was pleased to report that he personally conducted weekly lectures and conversations throughout the schools, while gymnastics was also introduced that school year. While "perhaps few of the boys need them for the exercise…many of the girls do, but it helps both [sexes] by [increasing] agility, precision and grace of movement—a healthy stimulus." There were 449 pupils enrolled in the schools, with an average attendance of 327; chronic absences concerned the school department's principal administrator. While there could be any number of reasons for attrition in school attendance, Alcott focused on the distractions of places of amusement, with the bowling alley and saloon singled out for special attention. This was enough of a problem that Alcott suggested to the selectmen of Concord that a separate school for troublesome boys be instituted, a school that would isolate the 12 to 20 boys who annoyed teachers and disturbed other pupils.

On November 6, 1860, Bronson Alcott strolled a few blocks to Concord center and voted in a presidential election for the first time. In his journal, he wrote, "At Town House, and cast my vote for Lincoln and the Republican candidates generally—the first vote I ever cast for a president and state officers." Statewide, Lincoln captured 63 percent of the vote, while his chief rival, Stephen Douglas, came in second with 20 percent of the vote. Upon hearing of a probable smashing victory in Massachusetts, Lincoln commented with wit that it was "a clear case...of the Dutch taking Holland."[6] This was to be the most geographically distorted vote in American political history, with Lincoln receiving 54 percent of the vote in the North and West but only 2 percent in the South.

The day after the election, Massachusetts governor John A. Andrew predicted that the new administration would be a brilliant success. Meanwhile, in neighboring Cambridge, Harvard students cheered the "Rail-splitter's" victory by toasting one of their own, Robert Lincoln, now dubbed the "Prince of Rails." In Concord, Senator Charles Sumner acknowledged the Republican victory by marching with celebrants to the home of another notable antislavery figure, Waldo Emerson, and he referred to Lincoln's election as a historic "landmark" for the cause. Calling attention to Concord's 1775 "Shot heard 'round the world," Sumner declared that "this victory... will cause a reverberation that will be heard throughout the world."[7]

In his 1860–61 superintendent's report to the selectmen, Alcott labeled Lincoln the "Illinois Splitter-Elect" and described Concord boys playing their "snow game" pitted against make-believe Southern secessionists. A reader might interpret this early engagement as a snowball fight between "Billy Yank" and "Johnny Reb." Concord's John S. Keyes, a delegate at the Republican Convention in Chicago that nominated Lincoln, had prior experience as a sheriff, and he served as Lincoln's bodyguard at the inauguration. He was subsequently appointed a U.S. marshal by the president, accompanied Lincoln to Pennsylvania and was close by when Lincoln delivered the Gettysburg Address. In 1863, Keyes bought the Bullet Hole House on Monument Street and was a member of the 1875 Battle of Concord Anniversary Committee, as well as the town's 250th Anniversary Committee in 1885.

Chapter 3

"OLD CONCORD AWAKE"

The Call for Troops

After the outbreak of hostilities at Fort Sumter in April 1861, Massachusetts and Concord supported the war effort in significant ways. Close to 160,000 men from the state served in the army and navy during the four-year conflict, while the first organized units to respond to Lincoln's call to arms in April 1861 came from Massachusetts. Ultimately, dozens of regiments marched to war from this state, with Concord soldiers enrolled in virtually all of them. Of a total of 263 Medal of Honor recipients from the Bay State, 131 received the award for heroism in the Civil War. Massachusetts was a significant producer of ammunitions and supplies, with the Springfield Armory serving as a principal source of armaments. This was America's first and last national armory (1777–1968). Its model 1861 Springfield rifle, a Minié-type musket, was a supreme weapon, with more than 1 million produced during the Civil War. Additionally, the commonwealth and Concord made substantial contributions to relief efforts. Boston's Dorothea Dix founded the Army Nurses Bureau, while Henry Whitney Bellows organized the United States Sanitary Commission and Clara Barton's nursing efforts led to the establishment of the Red Cross. Locally, the Concord Soldier's Aid Society was formed by a women's benevolent group with a mission of supplying the needs of fighting soldiers.

Following the thunderous roar of cannon fire at Fort Sumter on April 12, the war was on; two days after the fall of Sumter, President Lincoln called for 75,000 volunteers for a three-month enlistment. Three months later, having recognized that ninety-day enlistments were inadequate, Lincoln issued a call for 300,000 to serve three-year enlistments, and in July 1862, Congress passed a law implementing the draft, with a provision allowing for the payment of $300 to avoid the draft ($13,500 in today's dollars).

In response to the assault on Sumter, Bay Staters "sprang to their muskets, their bank accounts and their pulpits to defend the Union cause."[8] The headline in one Boston newspaper read "The North United at Last," while a huge U.S. flag was raised in front of Garrison's *Liberator* office on Washington Street opposite Franklin, proudly fluttering on a 140-foot-tall staff. You were either with the flag or against it. The busy General Recruiting Office in Boston was at 14 Pitts Street, about where the Government Center is today. Recruitment posters called for "patriotic persons to enlist in the service of their country. Pay and rations will begin immediately upon enlistment…feel pride in the supremacy which the Old Bay State enjoys in the contest for the Union and the Constitution. Do not withhold your sons from the conflict… though their blood may be dearer to you than your own…the cause is worth any sacrifice." The commonwealth promised to pay $12 per month to a family of three if the town requested assistance and, in addition, provided enlistment bounties of $100.

Chapter 4

Civil War Concord

On to Bull Run

In Concord, the Town House served as the recruitment center, with an enlistment table set up at the bottom of the stairs on the first floor. The new Town House, constructed in 1851, featured a town hall to be used for public meetings and functions. The building also contained two classrooms and a room for a town library. On April 22, 1861, a committee charged with the task of recruiting volunteers posted this broadside in the Town House:

WAR! WAR! WAR! VOLUNTEERS WANTED

To the patriots of Concord and vicinity. All those desirous of serving their country in this time of her need are hereby notified that a Company is to be raised in Concord and vicinity for that purpose…none but men of good and true and who are willing to be ready for any emergency, at a moment's notice, need apply!

Signed: Ephraim Wales Bull, Edwin Wheeler, Nathan Hosmer, Louis Surette, John Moore and Samuel Staples—Committee.

On October 17, 1862, George A. Hartshorn journeyed to the Town House and signed the enlistment paper, which was endorsed by Nathan B. Stow and A.G. Fay, selectmen of Concord. Subsequently, another document was signed by Captain Richard Barrett of the Concord Artillery on the same date, confirming that Hartshorn was mustered into service. Private

City hall (Town House), Concord, Massachusetts, 1875. *Concord Free Public Library.*

Hartshorn was assigned to Company G, 47th Massachusetts Volunteer Militia, commanded by Captain Barrett. Barrett was a Concord lumber dealer before the war and owner of the Barrett Farm from 1844 to 1852, and upon sale of the farm, he became treasurer of Middlesex Mutual Fire Insurance in Concord Center. Hartshorn would be joined by hundreds of others, all enrolling at the Town House.

In April 1907, a town-appointed committee began the task of identifying Union soldiers who had in Concord a birthplace or, prior to 1868, a home or grave. Three Civil War veterans served on this committee: George F.

Right: George Hartshorn enlistment document, October 17, 1862. *Author's collection.*

Below: Captain Richard Barrett endorses Hartshorn's enlistment, October 17, 1862. *Author's collection.*

Wheeler, Edward J. Bartlett and George F. Hall. Hall died during the research but was credited with providing a strong memory of men and events, work truly valued by his former comrades in arms. Their final report, "Soldiers and Sailors of Concord Massachusetts," was offered as a tribute to the brave men who have the honor of claiming Concord as their birthplace, home or grave. Ultimately, they compiled the names of more than 450 men who served from 1861 to 1865 as soldiers or sailors. These men served in sixty-three Massachusetts regiments, as well as regimental units from New York, Ohio, Maine, Illinois, Michigan, Missouri, New Hampshire, Vermont, Colorado and Wisconsin. In addition, Concord officers enlisted in the 6th, 37th and 75th United States Colored Troops, as well as the 118th United States Colored Troops Regiment.

The Battle of Bull Run

On April 17, 1861, a broadside was posted around town with this message:

War! War! War!

The Freemen of Old Concord will meet at the Town Hall on Friday evening, April 19th at 7½ O'Clock to take measures to fill up the ranks and strengthen the arms of the Concord Artillery Company, that they may go forth to fight our country's battles as our fathers did in '75. Come One! Come All! From the farm and the workshop, the counting room and the office, and show by our action that we are not degenerate sons of brave sires.

This 5th Massachusetts Volunteer Militia, known as the Concord Artillery, was the first to go from Concord to war, leaving town on a patriotic date that echoes 1775—April 19. Departing Boston as Company A, they were now eighty-two strong, becoming Company G upon arrival in the nation's capital. Under command of Captain George L. Prescott, they encountered Rebel fire at the Battle of Bull Run, July 21, 1861. They served their country for the initial mandated period of three months, returning to Concord with the loss of five of their number, all of whom were taken prisoner at Bull Run: William S. Rice, Cyrus Hosmer, William Bates, Edward S. Wheeler and Henry Wheeler. A citizens' fund of $5,000 was allotted to aid the soldiers and their families, and a ladies committee was formed to supply these fighting men with much-needed materials.

Raised by voluntary enlistment, the Concord Artillery was created by the Massachusetts Senate in 1804 and provided with two brass field pieces, which were exchanged for brass cannons in 1846. As a result of militia reorganization, the Concord Artillery, while retaining its name, was converted into an infantry unit in 1855, with the cannons remaining in the town's possession. In United States service beginning on May 1, 1861, the company was mustered out of service on July 31, with eighty-two men, a majority from Concord, having served in Company G.

The ladies of the town, rallying to assist Company G, reorganized in October 1861, becoming the Concord Soldier's Aid Society and pledging themselves to engage in assisting soldiers for the duration of the war. This benevolent organization consisted of more than 150 women and some men, with prominent families in the ranks: Emerson, Thoreau, Alcott,

WAR! WAR! WAR!

The Freemen of Old Concord will meet

AT THE

TOWN HALL,

On Friday Evening, April 19th,

AT 7 1-2 O'CLOCK,

to take measures to fill up the ranks and strengthen the arms of

THE CONCORD ARTILLERY COMPANY,

that they may go forth to fight our country's battles as our fathers did in '75.

Come one! Come all!! From the farm and the workshop, the counting room and the office, and show by our action that we are not degenerate sons of brave sires.

CONCORD, April 17, 1861.

April 19, 1861. "War! War! War!" *Concord Free Public Library.*

William Rice's grave. He was taken prisoner at Bull Run. *Author's collection.*

Sanborn, Hosmer, Hoar, Bartlett and Keyes. Initially, they met in the Town House, then the First Parish vestry and, later on, the Engine House near the train depot. Over the course of three and a half years, meticulous minutes of meetings were retained by the society's secretary. From 1861 to 1865, every member's name was recorded in the book, with annual dues of twenty-five cents listed next to each name. In addition to dues, the group raised money through donations, church collections, tea parties, theatrical productions and other benefits.

While Concord's men marched to Manassas, thirty-one miles southwest of Washington, D.C., 150 women gathered in the meeting hall on the second floor of the Town House and began to plan their contributions to Company G. The first order of business focused on designing an appropriate uniform for the Concord Artillery, ultimately resulting in a fatigue-patterned suit, which was deemed most desirable by company officers. Miss Harriette Moore, secretary for the ladies group, indicated that John Keyes was asked to inquire at headquarters for the material and pattern, with authorization to purchase it if requested. On May 1, 1861, the Concord Soldier's Aid Society sent the following to Company G's commander, Captain George Prescott:

- seventy-two drill jackets in three distinct sizes
- mending materials
- seventy-two pairs of pants
- fourteen cotton shirts
- sixty-four wash towels
- seventy-two cakes of chemical soap, donated by Bronson Alcott
- a box of lead pencils from Mr. Thoreau's shop

- cloth given by Mrs. Emerson
- six pairs of stockings
- some twenty or more daily newspapers
- four bundles of sponges
- seventy-five handkerchiefs

Beyond meeting the needs of the Concord Artillery, the ladies of town responded to urgent requests from the U.S. Sanitary Commission in Washington, ultimately resulting in shipments of clothing, medical supplies, food and other comfort items benefitting soldiers served by the commission. Within short order, a shipment left the Concord Depot destined for the nation's capitol, with the following boxed articles:

- blankets
- one quilt
- one bundle of linen sheets
- one bundle of books
- one pair of slippers
- two checkerboards (so popular that many more were sent)
- fourteen cushions
- one bag of dried apples
- one bedpan
- two shawls
- seventy-four pillowcases
- one cap
- four kegs of pickles (carried by Mr. Adams)

From October 1861 to October 1862, the Concord Soldier's Aid Society donated 14,146 articles to the Concord Artillery, the U.S. Sanitary Commission and military hospitals in Philadelphia and St. Louis, resulting in grateful letters of thanks. Included in these packages sent during the first year of the war, there were 8,792 rolls of bandages, so well made by Concord women and schoolchildren that one surgeon referred to them as "Concords." One of the most enthusiastic volunteers in this industrious organization was Grindall Reynolds, minister of First Parish Church. He packed boxes, wrote letters, knew the story of every Concord soldier and engaged in "winding miles of bandages."

Collectively, Concord sent twenty thousand bandages, enough if unrolled to stretch from Boston to Fitchburg; during the life of the war, forty thousand different articles were sent from Concord to the battlefield, hospitals and perhaps to Concord's Louisa Jane Barker. The wife of Reverend Stephen Barker, chaplain of the Massachusetts Heavy Artillery, Louisa joined the U.S. Sanitary Commission and was described by the organization as "one of the most earnest, useful and indefatigable of the Sanitary Commission in Washington." Daughter of William Whiting, antislavery activist and sister of Lincoln's solicitor of the War Department, Louisa and the family lived at the corner of Main Street and Academy Lane.

Reverend Grindall Reynolds's grave, Sleepy Hollow. *Author's collection.*

Edwin Shepard Barrett was born in Concord in 1833, served with distinction in the Civil War and, tragically, tumbled to an inglorious death in 1898. A great-great-grandson of Colonel James Barrett, commander of the Concord Minutemen and militia units at the North Bridge on April 19, 1775, Barrett was president of the Massachusetts Society of the Sons of the American Revolution. During the Battle of Bull Run, he was a volunteer attached to the staff of Colonel Samuel Lawrence, who commanded the 5th Massachusetts Regiment. Barrett carried orders on the field and later wrote an account of the battle that included an observer's view of the movements and actions of the Concord Artillery. At the twenty-fifth anniversary of the Battle of Bull Run, before an audience that included veterans of the Concord Artillery, Barrett delivered an address in the hall of the Concord Town House. Titled "What I Saw at Bull Run," the speech was later published in pamphlet form by Beacon Press.

Barrett's account of the Concord Artillery's road to war was supplemented by that of Charles Bowers, who at the age of forty-six was mustered into the Concord Artillery on May 1, 1861. Bowers had drafted a letter to the adjutant-general of Massachusetts, expressing his fervent belief "in the doctrine vindicated at the Old North Bridge in 1775, that resistance to tyrants is obedience to God; in this hour of our country's peril, I offer my services in her defense."[9] A father of six when he volunteered, he became a third lieutenant in Company G. When his three-month enlistment expired, he returned home and recruited another company, reenlisting with the 32nd Massachusetts Volunteers. Discharged for disability in 1863, his two oldest sons, William and Charles, also served, with Charles Jr. eventually succumbing to wounds he had suffered on the Gettysburg Battlefield.

In his archival memories of the Concord Artillery, Charles Bowers Sr. described the transport of the company from Concord to Boston and on to Washington, D.C. Leaving on April 19, the company arrived in Boston at 3:00 p.m. and proceeded to Faneuil Hall, where the soldiers occupied a room with four other companies. Active in both antislavery and temperance causes, Bowers was troubled by the liberal "potations of bad whiskey" that prompted some young men to engage in rude and noisy behavior while they were unpacking and distributing military equipment. When it came time for the train to slowly depart the Old Bay State, Bowers took note of the large number of men, women and children who gathered to wish the soldiers "God-speed" on their mission. Bells rang throughout Boston, and cannons were fired; "ladies shook our hands as if we were betrothed lovers." The troops' arrival in New York City was welcomed with still more excitement;

streets were packed with throngs of demonstrative, patriotic crowds. At the wharf, the boat was loaded with seven hundred men and eighty horses of the artillery, destined for Fort Munroe. After anchoring at Chesapeake Bay, the men marched to the depot at Annapolis, where the train was to convey them to Washington.

If the Concord Artillery was the first company to leave Concord, the 6th Massachusetts Volunteer Militia was the first completely outfitted Union regiment to reach the nation's capital. Its ranks included a twenty-year-old private from Concord. Hiram Wheeler was mustered into service on April 22, 1861, rotating out on August 2 upon completion of his three-month enlistment. The 6th Massachusetts was summoned to Boston by Special Order No. 14, issued on April 15. On the evening of the seventeenth, they entrained to Washington, and while traveling into Baltimore, a hotbed of secessionist activity, they were set upon by a tumultuous pro-Southern mob known as "Plug Uglies," their name being derived from plug hats they wore, as well as the spikes imbedded in the toes of their shoes to cause wounds with each kick. Four members of the unit were killed, with thirty-six wounded, and among the volunteers rushing to assist the fallen was Clara Barton of Oxford, Massachusetts, future founder of the American Red Cross. In a letter written to a family member, a young Acton soldier described this "Baltimore Riot of 1861" as "quite a little brush," but upon firing at the mob and killing fourteen Rebel sympathizers, others "scattered."[10] Shortly after arrival in Washington, members of the 6th paid respects to President Lincoln, visiting with him in the Executive Mansion. Mr. Lincoln thanked them for their service, indicating that they were the only regiment then in the city fully prepared to defend the capital.

Upon arrival in Washington, the boys of the 5th and 6th Massachusetts Regiments may well have internalized Charles Dickens's description of our nation's capital as "a city of magnificent intentions." With a population of seventy-five thousand in 1861 and surely a valued Federal symbol, Washington was an unfilled vision of national grandeur. Soldiers on pass, touring the center of government, would have been somewhat impressed with the boastful splendor of the White House, the Capitol, the Treasury Building, the U.S. Patent Office and the Smithsonian. However, barely habitable ramshackle wooden buildings dominated unhealthy neighborhoods above and below Pennsylvania Avenue. Lincoln's personal secretary, John Hay, a master wordsmith, had it right when he described Civil War Washington as "a congeries of hovels, inharmoniously sewn with temples." The Old City Canal, just south of the President's House, was a fetid sewer, emitting "a thousand stinks." In conjunction with crude sanitation systems, open drainage, pestilence and malaria-prone summers, this led to significant cases of dysentery, typhoid and cholera. Pennsylvania Avenue, designed as an expansive thoroughfare connecting the legislative and executive branches, was pocked with ruts and hollows—it was constantly overwhelmed with blowing dust during dry periods and was home to slop pits following rainstorms.

Washington was a city of contradictions, with an active group of abolitionists living in a thriving area for slavery and the slave trade. The 1860 population of 75,000 included 48,000 free colored persons and 3,687 slaves in the capitol; few exercised care in distinguishing free from slave. Concord soldiers bivouacking in the city in 1861 were no doubt surprised, if not appalled, to see newspaper advertisements announcing "NEGROES FOR SALE," with slave traders conducting major slave auctions within "slave jails" just above Pennsylvania Avenue. Washington was a dangerous place for blacks, and it would be another year before slavery would be abolished by Federal law throughout the district.

With Lincoln's call for seventy-five thousand troops to protect the nation's capital, the Concord Artillery and others with the 5th and 6th Massachusetts, combined with regiments from New York and Pennsylvania, quickly turned the city into a military town filled with young soldiers in blue. The Ancient and Honorable Concord Artillery, under the command of Captain George L. Prescott, was quartered in the Treasury Building. While camping in these ornate halls or walking the grounds of the Executive Mansion, soldiers on pass who could afford the price might have enjoyed a fine brunch at the crown jewel of Pennsylvania Avenue, the Willard Hotel. The late-morning menu included Chesapeake crabs, sea-turtle soup, oysters, roast pigeons, fresh shad and pig's feet, followed by imported cigars and fine whiskey.

While the serious-minded soldiers toured the Smithsonian, a center of culture established "for the increase and diffusion of knowledge among men," those looking for other excitement might have explored Washington's underground. Army camps were located nearby Swampoodle, a shantytown just north of the present Union Station, an area that attracted gamblers, hustlers, pickpockets and con artists, all of whom exploited boys in blue. Additionally, there were dozens of drinking places in Center Market (current site of the National Archives) and an estimated five thousand prostitutes in the city. At the time, the army's provost marshal listed 450 registered brothels in Washington.

The 5th Massachusetts, mustered into United States service on May 1, prepared for departure from Washington and subsequent encampment in Virginia by crossing the Potomac River via the Long Bridge. The soldiers settled in near Alexandria at Camp Andrew (named for their governor, John Andrew), on May 23, and eleven days later, they went to Camp Massachusetts, even closer to Alexandria. The newly promoted captain, George Prescott of the former Company A, now Company G, and the eighty-two men under his command in the Concord Artillery were introduced to new uniforms, discarding the soiled, worn clothing they left home with in April. Fitting soldier to uniform presented challenges, as a thin man may well have been given a uniform for a stockier soldier, while a tall man attempted to fit into a uniform for a five-foot-six individual. Eventually, it all seemed to work out satisfactorily, and the men of Company G enjoyed the new look. The company engaged in daily drills, with required time on picket and guard duty, and sporadic nighttime firing was a rude reminder that an enemy picket line was close by, requiring constant vigilance.

Concord's Edwin Barrett, in service as a volunteer, found the Concord Artillery encamped just outside Alexandria and lost no time reconnecting with men he grew up with, most particularly his boyhood friend Captain Prescott. He watched the company drilling, keeping up with writing letters home and generally adapting well to the routine of camp duties. He recalled meeting up with Vice President Hannibal Hamlin at Falls Church, who expressed strong interest in seeing a Rebel picket up close, and he did. Complaining bitterly of eating salt beef and hardtack, Barrett accompanied Lieutenant Charles Bowers and Private James Garty to the City Hotel in Alexandria, where they enjoyed a fine Fourth of July dinner, a welcome departure from the staple camp diet. The 5th celebrated Independence Day in camp, with the regimental chaplain reciting the Declaration of Independence, followed by a speech by Colonel Lawrence and a resounding rendition of "The Star-Spangled Banner," sung by the entire regiment.

At the "Re-Union of the Veterans of Co. G [Concord Artillery]" in 1886, Barrett spoke of his affection and respect for his childhood friend Captain Prescott, whom he visited often in camp, frequently sharing his tent and sleeping under the same blanket. He went on to say that Prescott treated him "with as much care and consideration as though I had been his own son. In fact, the same fatherly care was exercised toward every man under his command." The captain's superiors knew that he was a reliable officer, dedicated to task while maintaining a watchful eye in his devotion to soldiers of Company G. Barrett's praise for Prescott's leadership skills was echoed by that of Dr. Samuel Howe, who referred to Company G's commanding officer as "the stalwart man, every inch of whose six feet is of soldier stamp."[11] In his letter to Governor Andrew, Howe informed the governor that Prescott rejects hotel dinners, taking all meals with his men and eating only what they eat. He was a strong commander on duty but their considerate friend when off duty.

Edwin Barrett related an incident that demonstrates Prescott's commitment to all of the men in the 5th Massachusetts. A soldier in another company received a mortal wound, and while he suffered for several days, Captain Prescott devoted a great deal of time to caring for the "boy." On the night of his death, Prescott returned to his tent and, with tears in his eyes, informed Barrett that the boy was dead.

Rising through the ranks, Prescott was commissioned colonel in the 32nd Massachusetts Volunteers in December 1862. Following Bull Run, he took part in the battles at Fredericksburg, Chancellorsville, Gettysburg (where he was wounded), Rappahannock Station and Cold Harbor, as well as in the Wilderness campaign. On June 18, 1864, the 32nd crossed the James River near Petersburg, charging the Rebels and driving the enemy across an open field. In this advance, Colonel Prescott was mortally wounded, succumbing to this wound the next day. Colonel George Lincoln Prescott was interred in a place of honor on what became Author's Ridge in Sleepy Hollow, laid to rest close to the Emersons, Hawthornes, Alcotts and Thoreaus.

Of the men in the Concord Artillery, Barrett stated that with a strong devotion to duty and great love of country, no company in the regiment was more superior or better prepared to engage the enemy. On July 16, an order

Colonel George Prescott's grave. *Author's collection.*

was issued to the division to attack the Rebels at Manassas. Barrett reported that the 5th Massachusetts was at the head of the Union column, with the Concord Artillery at the immediate right of the regiment preparing for the onward march. The regiment marched ten miles, occasionally exchanging shots with mounted Rebels, who were always "prancing" in their front. Bivouacking for the night in an open pasture, campfires were lit while men attempted to consume the daily ration of hardtack ("trying to false teeth") and corned beef, described by the Concord Company as "salt horse." The troops had no tents, but curling up in blankets, they slept fitfully under an open sky as regimental pickets were constantly exchanging shots with enemy pickets.

Washington received the news of an impending battle at Manassas with great joy—so much so that there was a rush on the part of civilians to obtain passes to Virginia in order to witness the engagement. Saddle horses, carriages, wagons and hacks were rented, and the demand for picnic lunches was strong. Hotels and cooks provided "hampers of provisions" and wine, ordered at escalated prices to enjoy at "the military picnic" attended by gaily dressed celebrants. The gathering of spectators was confident of a victory within hours. After all, with thirty-five thousand troops, Brigadier General Irvin McDowell had organized the largest army ever assembled in North America. At the White House, Lincoln's sons Willie and Tad, along with two of their "Bucktail" playmates, had constructed a fort on the roof of the mansion, "firing" at Confederates across the Potomac.

On the day before the battle, the Concord Artillery was still in camp when the men heard of the order to make ready for a 2:30 a.m. departure on Sunday. Edwin Barrett informed his 1886 audience at the Town House that "there was not much sleep that night; the hum of preparation and expectancy seemed to pervade the vast camp and the thought of what the morrow might bring, forced itself upon the minds of all." At two o'clock in the morning, the drum sounded throughout camp, and very quickly, more than thirty thousand men stood ready for battle. However, this battle was lost before it was fought.

The original Union plan called for an attack on Friday, but the two-day delay allowed General Johnston to move the whole of his Confederate forces, thirty-two thousand strong, into Manassas before the Sunday battle. The general engagement began around 10:00 a.m., with the Concord Artillery and the other units in the 5th marching on the double-quick. Barrett initially remained on higher ground, where he could observe the battle below, but he moved away from this elevated ground when it became too dangerous.

Instead, relying on his skills climbing trees on Ponkatassett Hill in Concord, he elected to climb a persimmon tree, from which he had an unobstructed view. As he ascended the tree, he noticed that the tree had been pocked with Rebel bullets (and added to while he was perched on a branch). From this vantage point, during his two-hour stay, he watched any number of wounded men passing underneath. Leaving the tree, he passed within range of enemy fire, and when a spent ball rolled over the ground toward him, he foolishly stuck out his foot to stop it, though a soldier pulled him back. Simultaneously, a bullet grazed his ear, producing a sharp, burning sensation.

Following the battle, Barrett "found in these woods the ground literally covered with the corpses of the enemy," viewing close to fifty Rebels within a single span of fifty to sixty yards. Seeing this, he felt sure that the Union army had prevailed on the battlefield, but to his utter astonishment, he saw the entire panic-stricken army in retreat and from the summit said, "I compare it to nothing more than a drove of cattle." Among the units covering retreat for the 5th was the 8th New York Infantry, which included in its ranks a twenty-eight-year-old wagoner and bugler in Company D, Frederick Frese.

From the War Department, next to the Executive Mansion, President Lincoln received a telegram from an army captain of engineers that read: "The day is lost, save Washington and the remnants of the Army." Bull Run was a solid Union defeat.

With Yankees fleeing from the battlefield in a retreat that became a rout, so too did picnickers in party dresses who had been sipping champagne from the hillside, watching the carnage below. They were stunned to discover that this was a brutal defeat for the Union army on a blood-soaked field of battle. First Bull Run shocked the nation and marked the end of the age of innocence. Union casualties numbered 3,000 killed, wounded and missing, with 2,000 Rebel casualties. Putting this number in perspective, only 1,733 U.S. soldiers had been killed during the entire Mexican-American War. Walt Whitman, whose circle of admirers included Emerson, Thoreau and Bronson Alcott, would write, "Death is nothing here." War had struck home, no longer a distant abstraction. While at the headquarters hospital, Barrett observed "loads of wounded being brought up, with blood trickling from the ambulances like water from an ice cart, and directly in front of the church was a large puddle of blood."

With 70 percent of battlefield injuries causing wounds to extremities, the most common Civil War surgery was amputation, quite often the result of the slow-moving Minié ball, which produced horrific injuries. This soft-lead bullet could kill at one thousand yards, producing gaping holes, splintering bones and destroying muscles and tissues. Grooves in the bullet carried bacteria, which could produce infection resulting in amputation. The inch-long slug expanded when fired and spun at great speed from the rifle barrel's grooves, and with its spin, it could fly truer and travel farther with great accuracy. In treating battlefield injuries, the U.S. Surgeon General referred to Civil War medicine as "at the end of the medical Middle Ages." With Bull Run as a beginning, it is estimated that there were sixty thousand amputations on both sides during the war, and with no time to conduct labor-intensive surgical repairs, amputation was the expedient means employed to try to save a life. This procedure, conducted in about twelve minutes by surgeons earning the tag "Old Sawbones," was not done antiseptically; they utilized non-disinfected instruments, with little attention paid to hand washing before proceeding. As a result, there was a high mortality rate from both surgery and infections. Beyond the human casualties, Barrett reported that four thousand muskets, four thousand accoutrements and twenty-seven cannons were lost to the enemy. In the 5th Regiment, eight were killed, including one member of the Concord company, Robert Pemberton of Woburn.

Five members of the Concord Artillery were taken prisoner the day after the battle: William Sidney Rice, William C. Bates, Cyrus Hosmer, Henry L. Wheeler and Edward S. Wheeler. While retreating from the battlefield, these men were captured in the underbrush and initially incarcerated at Libby Prison in Richmond, where they remained for five months. In September, they were transferred to New Orleans and held at the "Old Parish Prison" until February; then they were dispatched to Salisbury, North Carolina, where they remained until exchanged for Rebel prisoners. Having been in Confederate prisons for close to a year, they were sent to New York's Governors Island via Washington. Edwin Barrett met them there, informing them of news from home. The major setback at Bull Run had alarmed Concordians, having heard that the battle at Bull Run had, in Barrett's words, "cut the Concord Company to pieces."

Henry Wheeler, born and raised in Concord, was in Company G when he was taken prisoner on July 21. Upon his enlistment in Concord, he drilled with a recruiting company in the Town House and was elected lieutenant by the men with whom he trained. He subsequently went to Washington, linking up with the Concord Artillery. Described by his brother George in "Memories of Concord Veterans" as "imperturbable" and possessing a "good nature," he managed to establish a connection with a prison guard at Salisbury and, with ingenuity, acquired small tools to establish a craft industry. Gaining access to bones before slaughtered animals were oiled, he carved penholders, rings and other articles from the bones. Eventually, he recruited other prisoners to assist with this craftwork, all intended to relieve the monotony of imprisonment. His confinement, along with the four others from the Concord Artillery, lasted almost a year. Upon their return to Concord, the men were welcomed with full civic honors as they were escorted by the Concord Artillery through the center of town. Sampson Douglas Mason (1805–1878), scion of a prominent Concord family and owner of a home at Meriam's Corner, delivered an address celebrating the "return of the prisoners of 5th Regiment, Company G at Concord"; portions of this address are excerpted here:

Hosmer and Rice, the Wheeler's-two,
With Bates the call obey,
And forty more brave men and true,
While Prescott leads the way.
You left this loved time honored town,
So framed in history's page,
Whose deeds of valor and renown
Survive from age to age.
And now, while here tonight with joy,
We welcome your return,
Some father's heart will miss his boy,
Some mother mourns her son,
Some brothers weep, some friends deplore
And wait and weep in vain,
Homeward their steps return no more,
They are—among the slain.
All honor to the living too,
Those who escaped the field;
They fought the fight, were brave and true,
Returning with their shield.
And you, long absent patriot band,
For whom our prayers have risen,
We grasp you warmly by the hand
And welcome you from prison.
We hail you from that Southern land
Where kindled treason's flame,
Which soon will be a smoking brand
Of blackness and of shame.

For Freedom in her onward march
Shall span our land once more,
And like the bow in heaven's blue arch,
Extend from shore to shore.
Then will the dove return again
With the olive branch of peace,
To reunite our severed chain,
And war and slavery cease.

During the time these men of Company G were held captive in Southern prisons, citizens in Concord raised $5,000 to aid their families. Over the course of the war, Concord citizens raised a total of $20,000 to support soldiers and their families. Henry Wheeler later joined the 47th Massachusetts in "Second Service of the Concord Artillery" from September 1862 to September 1863, and following that stint, he became brevet major in the 96th U.S. Colored Troops.

Following the major Union setback at Bull Run, Congress convened an extra session on July 22 and passed an act that authorized President Lincoln to recruit an additional 500,000 volunteers, the number to be furnished by the several states according to the Federal population. In response to that, Governor Andrew expressed his desire that the Massachusetts regiments be commanded by the best-educated and most experienced officers available, with no regard to political influence. It was the governor's desire to encourage many of those who had enlisted for three months, and were now discharged, to reenlist in the new volunteer regiments. Jacques Gowing, born in Concord near Merriam's Corner, formerly called Gowing's Corner, became a reenlisted veteran by joining the 21st Massachusetts Volunteers in August.

Another new recruit, First Sergeant James Fernald, born in Portsmouth, New Hampshire, enlisted in Augusta, Maine, in August 1861 and served with the 7th Maine. He left for Baltimore on August 23 and was assigned to duty in that city until October 25, at which time he transitioned to Washington and then died at the age of twenty-seven on November 9, 1861, at a Baltimore hospital. Since his wife and son lived in Concord during his military service, James Fernald was laid to rest in Sleepy Hollow, the *first* Civil War soldier to be buried in Concord.

Closing out his volunteer service under Colonel Lawrence with the 5th Massachusetts, Edwin Shepard Barrett returned to Concord and became a successful Boston businessman. His wholesale leather business provided the financial resources for Barrett to build a house on sacred battleground on Liberty Street, land where his great-grandfather Colonel James Barrett and the Concord Minutemen gathered in 1775. He purchased the old eighteenth-century property of Captain David Brown from George Keyes, and as a self-proclaimed custodian of historic ground, he built himself a mansion, calling it Battle Lawn. On December 21, 1898, Barrett died at his residence, falling from a third-story window and hitting the pavement below. The *New York Times*' obituary reported that the fall occurred while he was attempting to open a window and went on to say that

James Fernald's grave. He was the first soldier of the Civil War buried in Concord. *Author's collection.*

the family revealed that Barrett had been subject to fainting spells. What was not reported at the time was information regarding Barrett's declining health and financial setbacks. In 1953, Battle Lawn was torn down by a future owner, Stedman Buttrick, six years before the National Park Service took title to the battleground. All that remains of Battle Lawn today is the brick entrance in the stone wall on Liberty Street. Visitors may look for flat terrain near where the flagpole is today to see the former site of Battle Lawn just behind the opening in the stone wall.

The 20th Massachusetts Volunteer Infantry, the "Bloody 20th," with twenty-three Concord enlistees, was in U.S. service from July 1861 to July 1864. Initially assembled at Camp Massasoit in Readville, this regiment later on carried the nickname "Harvard," since many of its officers were Harvard graduates. Of the ninety-three Harvard men who perished while serving the Union, eight were officers in the 20th, including the 1775 Midnight Rider's grandsons, Paul J. Revere and his brother, Edward H. Revere. This regiment became one of the most significant units in the Army of the Potomac, participating in most of the major battles of the war, beginning with Ball's Bluff, near Leesburg, Virginia, on October 21, 1861.

While considered a small engagement, the Ball's Bluff campaign was another Union rout, with 450 Federal casualties and 550 men captured by Confederates, including both Revere brothers. A serious miscalculation on the part of a Union commander allowed Rebel forces to organize, driving Yankee troops back across the Potomac. George Gray described this battle in his "Memories of Concord Veterans of the Civil War." A carpenter and house builder, Gray enlisted in Waltham and was attached to the 20th, while his family resided in Concord. Ball's Bluff was his initiation into war, an experience seared in his memory as a battle that resulted in heavy losses, "as many men tried to save themselves by jumping into the Potomac, but either drowned by their exertions, or were shot trying to cross." Paying tribute to his fallen comrades, Gray wrote of "sleeping that sleep that knows no awakening." Colonel Paul Revere and Assistant Surgeon Edward Revere spent several months in a Rebel prison in Richmond and were then exchanged for several Confederate "pirates." Five Concord soldiers in the 20th died during their wartime service, including Private Charles Brigham, who died on February 15, 1863, and is interred at Sleepy Hollow.

In the "stand and deliver" combat of the Civil War, officers who earned the respect and admiration of their soldiers were those who walked the line with their men, fully prepared to take the same risks as those they commanded. One of these officers in the 20th, Colonel Edward Baker, after whom President Lincoln had named his second son, was a U.S. senator from Oregon. All day during the Ball's Bluff engagement, Baker walked the line, monitoring the positioning of his troops and constantly providing words of encouragement. While continuing to cheer his troops and directing action against the enemy, Baker was struck by a sharp volley of bullets fired from the woods. Receiving wounds from eight bullets, he died "without a groan," becoming the only U.S. senator to be killed during the Civil War.

In the wake of another Union defeat, Congress created a Joint Committee on the Conduct of the War as an attempt to oversee decisions made by senior Union commanders on the battlefield. It was clear to everyone that this was now going to be a prolonged, bloody war. Following Bull Run and Ball's Bluff, Lincoln declared, "Neither party, expected for the war, the magnitude, or the duration, which it already attained."[12] Back in Concord, the board of selectmen's 1861–62 report began with these words: "The past year has been an eventful one. In the midst of an unparalleled prosperity, we have been plunged into Civil War—on the anniversary of that nineteenth of April, which was baptized in the blood of our fathers, our soldiers were called to arms for the defense of the capital."

On November 18, 1861, Julia Ward Howe—accompanied by Governor Andrew; her husband, Samuel; one of John Brown's six financial backers; and others—arrived at Washington, boarding at the Willard Hotel on Pennsylvania Avenue. Evidence of the war was seen all over the capital. According to her daughter, Florence, Julia was appalled by the "ghastly advertisement" of an embalming agency that specialized in cosmetic treatment for preserving soldiers' remains, as well as posted fees for forwarding the bodies of those who perished. In company with her traveling party, Julia witnessed a review of troops and was invited to speak to the 1st Massachusetts Heavy Artillery, a unit that included nine Concord soldiers, the three Melvin brothers among them. While listening to Union soldiers sing a rousing rendition of "John Brown's Body," Julia's minister, Reverend James Freeman Clark of King's Chapel in Boston, urged her to write more significant lyrics for the tune. Clark's coterie of Boston and Concord friends included Emerson, William Henry Channing, Oliver Wendell Holmes, Margaret Fuller and Theodore Parker. The original draft of what became the "Battle Hymn of the Republic" was scripted from her room at the Willard and later sold to the *Atlantic Monthly* for five dollars. In later life, Julia reflected on her career, and among her proudest moments was her recollection of a speaking engagement at Bronson Alcott's Concord School of Philosophy, when she "pleaded the cause for the slave" and assisted in the development of the women's suffrage movement.

Following Bull Run and Ball's Bluff, Governor Andrew issued a November Thanksgiving proclamation ensuring that the soldiers in the field were not forgotten. It was read to every Massachusetts regiment and was greeted with great cheer, as General Nathaniel Banks suspended military duty and religious service was conducted for men of the 5th Massachusetts. Eighty-three Concord soldiers in the 5th were beneficiaries of the dinner, which was summed up as follows:

95 turkeys, totaling 997½ pounds
76 geese, weighing 666 pounds
73 chickens, 165 pounds
95 Plum puddings, weighing in at 1,179 pounds

If you were to state the total dinner weight in pounds, it came to one and a half *tons.*

With the 5th Massachusetts and its Concord Artillery off to war, life at home was, in many ways, business as usual. In 1861–62, Concord's financial report to townspeople indicated the following:

- *The Town disbursed in aid of military volunteers families: $640.81* [$391 borrowed from the volunteers fund and $249.81 from the town treasury].
- *The Town appropriated $1720 toward the new Town House debt, which totaled $11,000.*
- *$1200 expended in repair of highways.*
- *$300 to repair bridges.*
- *$200 set aside for a factory engine for the fire department.*
- *$72.89 spent for kerosene lamps for the Town Hall and library in the Town House.*
- *$9.60 paid for lumber to repair the school houses.*
- *$100 paid A.B. Alcott—School Superintendent salary.*
- *$19 for care of clocks on school house and church* [official town clock].
- *$1.50 for rope for the Liberty Pole.*
- *$54.50 paid to Heman* [sic] *Newton for entertaining the Concord Artillery before heading to war on April 19th.*
- *$4 for Jonas Melvin for police services on July 4[th.]*
- *17 lots sold in the cemetery for $238.00.*
- *Cash on hand in the Town treasury: $176.57.*
- *Total cost of the high school for the year: $1124.20, which includes a total of $19.32 for books, chalk and incidentals.*

In the School Committee's report for 1861–62, the members lamented that "[o]ne fault of all the children now growing up is that they are too little subjected to reasonable authority, at school and at home…parents should not lessen the teachers already scanty authority." Regarding the role of teachers, the report continues: "The government of the schools is entrusted by law to the teachers, and they are expected to preserve strict order of discipline, and to pay constant attention to the language, the manners, and the conduct of the scholars in and about the schools."

During the first year, Massachusetts spent $3,384,649.88 on the war, with $987,263.54 reimbursed by the Federal treasury, leaving an unpaid balance of about $2.5 million. This excluded the amount paid by cities and towns in

Concord Center, south side, looking west, circa 1865. *Concord Free Public Library.*

the commonwealth for the support of families of soldiers, which amounted in the aggregate to $250,000.00, all of which was to be reimbursed by the state treasury and raised by direct taxation on the property in the state. Included in expenses was $500,000.00 for five thousand new Pattern 1853 Enfield rifle muskets to be purchased from England. The rifling in these muskets provided greater range and accuracy, but the bullet would *drop* rather than head directly to a target. In frenetic battle conditions, even an excellent marksman would have difficulty adjusting trajectory, speed and distance to hit the target.

Chapter 5

1862

Antietam and Fredericksburg

I n examining the Civil War by the numbers, 2.5 percent of the American
population died from battle wounds or war-related diseases from 1861 to
1865. There was a 20 percent death rate for all Civil War soldiers, with a
solid ratio of three to one in Confederate deaths to Union deaths. Among the
Union casualties, more than 100,000 corpses were found in the South through
a reinterment program from 1866 to 1869. Two out of every three Civil
War deaths came from disease. (Conservative Union figures were 110,000
from battle wounds and 225,000 from disease.) Regarding prisoners of war,
there were 193,743 Northerners and 214,865 Southerners held during the
war, with a 12 percent mortality rate in Northern prisons, compared to 15
percent dying in prisons in the South. Confederates could barely provide
food for their military, with little left for Union prisoners. Southern prisoners
fared better in the North due to better hospitals, physicians and medicine
and more plentiful foods.

Among those dying from disease was Private Herman Flint of Concord,
who at the age of eighteen enlisted in the 16th Massachusetts Volunteers on
July 13, 1861. As was the case with a majority of recruits, Flint had been
a farmer, cultivating his father's farm in Concord, but at the time of his
enlistment, he was working at a mill in North Chelmsford. Flint died in
Suffolk, Virginia, from chills and fever brought on by bathing in cold water
and reputedly was the first Concord man to die in the service. Since his body
was buried in Suffolk, Herman's father had a cenotaph erected for his son as
a tomb of honor in the family lot in Sleepy Hollow.

With perhaps 750,000 Union and Confederate deaths, as many as 300,000 Civil War soldiers remain unidentified today. Concord's Thomas Carey, who had worked for Charles Bowers, a shoemaker, enlisted in Company F, 2nd Massachusetts Volunteer Infantry, and died on August 9, 1862, from exhaustion while marching from Culpeper to Cedar Mountain, Virginia. Private Carey is presumably buried near where he fell. With about thirty Union-Confederate skirmishes and full battles on Virginia soil, the total number of casualties in that state was horrific. (There were 152,000 Union casualties in just the battles of Bull Run, Fredericksburg, Spotsylvania, Petersburg and the Wilderness.) During the spring 1862 campaign, Brigadier General (and future president) James Garfield said this of the war: "The horrible sights that I have witnessed on this field, I can never describe. No blaze of glory that flashes around the magnificent triumphs of war, can ever atone for the unwritten and unutterable horrors of the scene of carnage."[13]

Garfield commanded the U.S. Army of the Ohio, with Concord's Private Charles Wright serving in his 11th Ohio Volunteers and being killed on September 17, 1862, at Antietam. An early hometown battlefield casualty, Wright is buried at Concord's hallowed ground, Sleepy Hollow Cemetery, more than likely named after Washington Irving's "The Legend of Sleepy Hollow." The hollow, purchased by the town, was brought into the older cemetery in 1855. Emerson delivered the address on dedication day, penning these words: "This is the garden of the living as well as the dead…when these acorns that are falling from our feet, are oaks overshadowing our children in a remote century, this mute green bank will be full of history: the good, the wise and the great will have left their names and virtues on the trees." Three decades later, Emerson was laid to rest on that ridge.

Concord's cemetery records indicate that there are at least 157 Civil War veterans buried at Sleepy Hollow, many of whom are identified by "U.S. Civil War Veteran" markers. Prior to Sleepy Hollow's designation as a final resting place, Nathaniel Hawthorne and his wife, Sophia, enjoyed lingering in the shade there, with Hawthorne describing his dream of building a castle on what is now Author's Ridge. The Civil War, according to Sophia, oppressed her husband, a man who experienced no evil in his life but saw and sorrowed over evil. In 1862, Hawthorne met with President Lincoln in the White House and subsequently wrote an article in the *Atlantic Monthly* following his return to Massachusetts:

> [The president] *was dressed in a rusty black frock-coat and pantaloons, unbrushed, and worn so faithfully that the suit had adapted itself to the*

curves and angularities of his figure, and had grown to be an outer skin of the man. He had shabby slippers on his feet. His hair was black, still unmixed with gray, stiff, somewhat bushy, and had apparently been acquainted with neither brush nor comb that morning, after the arrangements of the pillow… his physiognomy is as coarse a one as you would meet anywhere.

Despite this unflattering physical description, Hawthorne genuinely liked Lincoln, praising his tact, wisdom, keen faculties and integrity. In May 1864, Hawthorne died in his sleep in New Hampshire while traveling with former president Franklin Pierce; his body was brought back to Concord to repose on the "mute green bank…among the good, the wise and the great."

Two years earlier, on May 6, 1862, Henry David Thoreau, age forty-four, succumbed to tuberculosis at his Main Street home in Concord. Four days later, the bell at First Parish Meetinghouse tolled forty-four times, honoring the life of this independent genius who knew and loved every acre of Concord. On the day of his funeral, Bronson Alcott dismissed the schools so that three hundred children could join the cortège, heading from the church into Monument Square, up Bedford Street and then proceeding into Sleepy Hollow. The *Boston Transcript* reported that townspeople and pilgrims from parts beyond followed the body to the grave, where it was "reverently lowered into the bosom of the earth." William Ellery Channing, Reverend Grindall Reynolds and R.W. Emerson were among the mourners saluting their fellow abolitionist. In Emerson's eulogy, he said of Thoreau:

He was bred to no profession; he never married; lived alone; he never went to church; he never voted; he refused to pay a tax to the state; he ate no flesh; he drank no wine; he never knew the use of tobacco; and though a naturalist, he used neither trap nor gun. He had no talent for wealth and knew how to be poor…but an idealist he was, standing for the abolition of slavery.

On the first anniversary of Thoreau's death, Bronson Alcott led another procession, this time to Walden Pond, where friend Henry had lived for the better part of two years. Gathering stones from the water and shoreline, the entourage walked the site of Thoreau's cabin and erected an improvised cairn in his memory. From the shores of Walden to the Battle of Shiloh shortly before he passed, Thoreau remained staunchly opposed to slavery while also advocating civil disobedience in a just cause.

George Phineas How was the son of Phineas How, who came to Concord in 1821, establishing a commercial trading business, Currier and How, which was located on the north side of Main Street. Young George attended grammar school in a building that became the Masonic Hall in Monument Square and later on clerked in his father's establishment. In 1851, he joined the Concord Artillery and, eleven years later, went to war with that unit, under the command of Captain Richard Barrett, in what was now the 47th Massachusetts Volunteers. How was subsequently promoted to sergeant major and stationed in New Orleans for ten months. Following his military service, he returned to Concord, resuming active membership in the First Parish Church; after what may have been the longest tenure in the Concord Artillery, twenty-five years, he resigned in 1875. In 1884, he took command of the Concord Post of the Grand Army of the Republic (GAR).

Following his father, Phineas, George joined Concord's esteemed men's organization the Social Circle. As a director of the Concord bank and a trustee of the Middlesex Institution for Savings, Phineas had joined this fraternal group in 1831, replacing John Adams, who in the words of John Keyes was "a very lazy man with an historic name…how he ever acquired means enough, or manifested energy enough to build a house, is a puzzle, unless the wife may have had more to do with it than the husband."[14] Concord's Social Circle was formed in 1794 with its original purpose intended to "strengthen social affections and disseminate useful communications among its members." Chartered to consist of no more than twenty-five members who were expected to engage in local politics and various spheres of influence in town, Emerson described the membership as "the solidest of men who yield the solidest of gossip." Writing in *Concord: Climate for Freedom*, Ruth Wheeler scolded the men in the Social Circle for making fun of the Female Charitable Society by calling it a "monthly sewing meeting" and a "chattable society." Wheeler informed her readers that the men's Social Circle "had NO other purpose but talk."

In July 1862, President Lincoln called for an additional 300,000 men to serve for three years, with Governor Andrew's quota for Massachusetts pegged at 15,000. The Town of Concord pledged to recruit 22, with $3,000 authorized by town vote to support this effort. (Bounty fees ranging from $100 to $150 were paid to enlistees.) On July 12, a Town Resolution was passed at a town hall meeting: "We hail with satisfaction the call of the president for 300,000 men…and pledge our lives and fortunes to the support of the Union and the suppression of the Rebellion."

Richard Barrett was born in the Heywood House on Lexington Road in 1818 and served in the Concord Artillery for forty years, acting as the unit's commander for half that time. At the outbreak of the war, he did not accompany the Concord Artillery to the front, but other officers went instead, with Lieutenant George Prescott commanding. This clearly did not sit well with some townspeople, and in 1862, Barrett transitioned, becoming captain of Company G in the 47th Massachusetts Volunteer Militia and being dispatched to New Orleans, serving under General Nathaniel Banks from September 1862 to September 1863. Upon returning to Concord, Barrett became a deputy U.S. marshal, followed by an appointment as secretary and treasurer of the Mutual Fire Insurance Company. Marshal John S. Keyes described Barrett as "predominately our soldier by his life-long interest in and devotion to the service."

ANTIETAM

The "Harvard Regiment," the 20th Massachusetts, included twenty-three Concord soldiers on the roster, five of whom were killed on the battlefield or died from disease. Charles Brigham died on February 15, 1863, and is buried at Sleepy Hollow. Edward Garrity, a Concord farmworker, enlisted on September 19, 1861, and died from chronic diarrhea in Virginia in October 1862, and one year later, his father, Malachi, enlisted in the same company his son had joined, the 20th's Company E. In Company B, Private Thomas Mack died from battle wounds in May 1864, while Company H lost Charles A. Mohr. In the bloodiest single day of the war, John McDonough, a former Concord laborer just nineteen when mustered, was killed on the Antietam Battlefield on September 17, 1862, and is interred in a garden of heroes at Antietam National Cemetery.

With the outcome a tactical draw, Antietam remains the most horrific day of combat anywhere, with twenty-five thousand Union and Confederate dead, wounded or missing. Entire regiments were wiped out in minutes during the deadly concentration of firepower over a twelve-hour period. Describing this engagement in his "Memories of Concord Soldiers," George Gray wrote:

> *There were dead of both armies, gathered together, laid in rows for burial; the ground was strewn with muskets, dismounted cannon, caissons and all kinds of munitions of war, as well as clothing, knapsacks and blankets. As the battle swayed back and forth, the debris was scattered all the way from Antietam Creek to the Dunker Church and Sharpsburg, a distance of about*

four miles. It was a desolate and appalling sight and brought sadness to the heart, to contemplate the destruction of human life, to say nothing of the property destroyed. Here was a line of dead that one might have walked for more than a half mile without stepping on the ground. All along the route was strewn the debris of battle.

Caring for more than eighteen thousand wounded soldiers following this one-day battle proved to be an imposing challenge for medical personnel operating in unsanitary conditions with limited medical equipment and unsterilized instruments. Every church, schoolhouse, barn and store for miles around was filled with the wounded. Thousands of amputations were performed, with an amputee facing a 35 percent risk of death from the surgery and only a 10 percent chance of surviving infection if it occurred afterward.

What accounted for this extensive lethality with staggering casualty rates on Civil War battlefields? Military tacticians and historians reviewing these engagements have concluded that it was attributable to the sheer volume of rifle volleys and bullets expended that killed and wounded large numbers of soldiers on both sides. It was not the marksmanship of the infantrymen; in fact, weapons instruction and target practice were not a primary component of training. About 90 percent of all wounds were caused by gunshot, with artillery shell fragments responsible for most of the remainder. In the aftermath of a battle at Stones River, General William Rosecrans calculated that 20,000 rounds of artillery fired had hit just 728 men, while *2 million* Union cartridges inflicted only 13,832 hits on the Rebels. Working the arithmetic, it required 27 cannon shots to inflict 1 artillery hit and 145 rifle shots to score 1 infantry hit.

Lee's army moved into Maryland, with forty thousand men coming up against eighty-five thousand in the Army of the Potomac. Each soldier carried on average sixty rounds and, with reloading, could fire two rounds per minute for thirty minutes. Soldiers would be resupplied two to three times on the battlefield. This resulted in a rain of bullets with a range of one-fourth of a mile or more, throwing enormous quantities of lead at one another. (The Springfield rifle musket could hit a man with a .58-caliber Minié ball as far away as five hundred yards.) Whether firing during frontal assaults or from a covered and concealed position, it didn't require accuracy. The firepower and range of all those rifles enlarged the killing zone, creating a deafening, thundering roll of musketry, ripping a closely packed regiment to pieces at some distance.

Regarding transportation and logistical support for an eighty-five-thousand-man Army of the Potomac traveling toward Antietam, General George McClellan's troops drew more than 100,000 pairs of shoes and boots, ninety-three thousand pairs of trousers and ten thousand blankets from supply depots. They had three thousand wagons, more than twenty-two thousand horses and ten thousand mules in their caravan. An individual soldier departing on campaign may have had sixty pounds of gear, including weapons, ammunition and a three-day food supply.

Major General George McClellan had raised and organized the Army of the Potomac and served as general-in-chief from November 1861 to March 1862. Accused by Lincoln of suffering from "the slow," he habitually overestimated the strength of the enemy, constantly requested thousands of additional troops and failed to move on Richmond. In the immediate aftermath of the standstill at Antietam, despite the president's urgent instructions, McClellan failed to pursue Robert E. Lee and the Army of Virginia. Lincoln's patience was exhausted, and on November 5, 1862, he relieved McClellan of his command. Three days later, Concord's George Gray witnessed the general's departure from the field, en route to Fredericksburg. In his memories of the moment, Gray wrote, "Soldiers turned out en masse to see their beloved general as he rode through camp with his staff to take his leave. Probably the Army of the Potomac never had a leader that had such care for his soldiers and was so beloved by them. Men shed tears."

At the same time McClellan was leaving the battlefield, Louisa May Alcott, growing weary of the "sewing bees and lint picks" conducted by the Concord Soldier's Aid Society, longed to see the war for herself. In her November diary, she wrote, "I decided to go to Washington as a nurse if I could find a place. Help is needed and I love nursing and must let out my pent-up energy in some new way. I long to be a man, but as I can't fight, I will content myself with working for those who can."

With her strong motivation to contribute to the war effort and join Dorothea Dix's nursing corps, Louisa departed for Washington in early December with instructions to report to the new Armory Square Hospital, but later on, she was assigned to the run-down Union Hotel Hospital in Georgetown known as the "Hurly-Burly House." At the time of the thirty-year-old writer's arrival, there were nearly sixty makeshift hospitals spread across Washington, many of them former churches, public buildings, schools, halls and homes, all commandeered by the military. Louisa was assigned to Ward 1, the entrance to which carried an old label that read

"Ballroom." Just three days after her arrival, the hospital was loaded with wounded soldiers pouring in from the battle at Fredericksburg. Stunned by the magnitude of so much suffering as the ambulances arrived at Union, she later described the "begrimed, frozen and shattered" soldiers. Her first patient, an Irishman, eased her discomfort when he asked to be washed, and inspired by his courage and resolve, she quickly adapted to the challenging but exhausting task. In her journal, she summarized her duties as "cutting up food for helpless boys, washing faces, dressing wounds...til it seems I would joyfully pay down all I possess for fifteen minutes rest." Writing to a friend in Concord, she related that she was "too occupied violently sewing patriotic blue shirts" to write more often.

These military hospitals were characterized as places to avoid, as discoveries in bacteriology and antiseptic medicine were still several years away. Typhoid, malaria and diarrhea swept through these unsanitary, crowded, poorly ventilated, damp and chaotic facilities. Functioning in these severe conditions, Louisa paid dearly for her volunteer service. Just six weeks after reporting for work at Union, working twelve-hour shifts, she contacted typhoid fever and was treated with mercury in the form of calomel. Calomel treatment was conducted via "heroic dosing," a drenching medical procedure, widely prescribed, that produced chronic mercury poisoning. These heavy doses caused hair and teeth to fall out. Following this exposure to mercury, Louisa suffered loss of hair and teeth, experienced delirium and had chronic bouts of shooting pains in her limbs for the remainder of her life.

In her journal, she summarized her ill health by writing, "I was never ill before this time and never well afterward." Having returned to Concord after her father traveled to Washington to bring her home and just weeks before the Battle of Gettysburg, Alcott wrote four installments of "Hospital Sketches" for *Boston Commonwealth*, an abolitionist newspaper. The

Louisa May Alcott's grave, Sleepy Hollow. *Author's collection.*

publisher paid her forty dollars for these submissions in book form and sold them for 50 cents apiece, with her royalty set at 5 cents per copy and another 5 cents donated to children orphaned by war. While creating fictional characters in these sketches, they remain truly authentic representations of her wartime experiences as a nurse.

FREDERICKSBURG

Reviewing 1861–62 campaigns leading up to the Battle of Fredericksburg, Massachusetts had been the first to reach Washington in April 1861 and the first to stake commonwealth colors in Virginia. Bay State regiments were the first to penetrate North Carolina in 1862, followed by campaigns in Mississippi and Louisiana. Before the year ended, they were to first to hit Texas soil. During the first six months of 1862, there were 4,587 new Massachusetts infantry recruits dispatched to the front, all enlisting for three years service. Massachusetts managed to furnish its prescribed quota of troops without resorting to the draft, which Governor Andrew and municipalities labored to avoid. Concord and other towns conducted active recruiting events, which included public meetings, speeches and designated "camps" to both examine and enroll recruits. In Boston, many merchants closed businesses in early afternoon so that the remainder of the day could be devoted to recruitment.

The adjutant-general wrote letter after letter to town officials throughout the commonwealth, calling on patriotic men to enlist at once and imploring important people in each town to raise the men, by whatever means necessary. Each recruit would be entitled to one month's pay (thirteen dollars) and a bounty of twenty-five dollars in addition, as soon as a company was full. The adjutant-general went on to say that if voluntary enlistment failed to meet mandated quotas, the draft might be the next step. Community quotas ranged from 29 for Rockport to 82 for Nantucket, 102 for Pittsfield and 212 for Haverhill. The main effort, consistent with the governor's desire, was to fill up regiments already in the field by sending large numbers of new recruits to established regiments. At length, the quota of the state was filled, with regimental transports shipped out of Boston Harbor.

From 1861 to 1865, there were fifty major battles and five thousand minor engagements, with 450 Concord soldiers representing eighty army infantry, artillery, cavalry and hospital units. When not in battle, which was three-fourths of the time, a Concord soldier's day would begin in camp with reveille at 5:00 a.m. in summer months and at 6:00 a.m. during the cold season. After breakfast, there might be five drills scheduled for the day, each one running one to two hours. If not training, men would clean camp, dig trenches for latrines, gather wood for fires, seek water and otherwise engage in some pleasure pursuits. Popular physical activities consisted of foot racing, wrestling, broad jumping, boxing, snowball fights and base ball. Since at that time a base runner had to be hit by a soft thrown ball or batted ball to be out, high-scoring games were quite common. In one game, the 13th Massachusetts, with seven Concord men on the roster, defeated the 104th New York team, 66–20. Soldiers also devoted time to writing letters home and reading popular publications of the day, which included the Bible, *Harper's Weekly*, *Frank Leslie's Illustrated Newspaper*, the classics and dime novels.

Troops welcomed listening to regimental brass bands, harmonicas and fiddles, while indulging in singing many patriotic and sentimental songs that stirred memories of home. Popular tunes and melodies ranged from "Yankee Doodle Dandy" and "John Brown's Body" to "Home Sweet Home" and "The Girl I Left Behind." The 45th Massachusetts developed a strong following for staging theatrical productions that might include an all-male cast dancing the Virginia reel or the cotillion. Around the evening campfire, men shared gossip, swapped stories and engaged in constant practical jokes. A more creative pursuit might involve carving smoking pipes from brier root or fashioning rings and ornaments from bones and wood.

Other means of relieving the boredom of camp life and escaping the tensions of battle were more raucous in nature, exposing the contradictions of the camp, which could be both virtuous and immoral. One soldier pronounced the experience as "the last place for me or any civil man." The temptations to vice and vile behavior consisted of card playing, gambling, swearing and drunkenness, often a result of drinking potent whiskey like "Old Red Eye" or mixing your own concoction consisting of bark juice, tar water, turpentine, brown sugar, lamp oil and alcohol. In addition, some soldiers relaxed by soliciting "horizontal refreshments," which might include visiting "Madame Russell's Bake Oven"—prostitutes were plentiful in war zones. The end result of their pleasures showed up in medical reports with 10 percent of soldiers in the Army of the Potomac being treated for venereal disease. It was long thought that the term "hookers" was derived from prostitutes following Major General Joe Hooker's brigade, but its usage predates Hooker's camp followers.

Sleeping accommodations were less than desirable, as Concord soldiers lived in canvas tents designed to accommodate twelve men, but in true military fashion, they became home to twenty. With little access to clean water for bathing purposes, this contributed to abysmal campground conditions.

Union army soldiers were well fed at the beginning of the war, with adequate daily rations of salt pork, beef, flour, beans, coffee, salt and sugar. Before the Battle of Fredericksburg in December 1862, the 20th Massachusetts, with more than twenty Concord soldiers in its ranks, cleared the way for the passage of the army across the river. Two Concord soldiers, Charles Brigham and John Williams, were members of Company K, commanded by Captain Allen Shepard. In an abstract of provisions sold to his company, this is what the commanding officer requisitioned for a sixty-day period:

19 lbs. of pork @ 9½ cents…$1.80 total
157¾ lbs. of fresh beef @ 7½ cents…$11.38¼
6 lbs. of salt beef @ 7 cents…42 cents
15 lbs. of ham @ 12 cents…$1.80
417 lbs. of flour @ 3⅓ cents…$13.90
63 lbs. of hard bread @ 4 cents…$2.52
13 quarts of beans @ 6¼ cents…81¼ cents
8 lbs. of rice @ 7 cents…56 cents
7 lbs. of hominy @ 2½ cents…17½ cents
5 lbs. of coffee @ 15 cents…75 cents
52 lbs. of sugar @ 9½ cents…$4.94
27 lbs. of candles @ 19 cents…$5.13
5 lbs. of soap @ 5 cents…25 cents
52 quarts of molasses @ 8 cents…$4.16
94 lbs. of potatoes @ 1 cent…94 cents

TOTAL……………$49.54

Despite this substantive requisition, when a regiment was on the move, supplies became limited, and foraging off the land was commonplace. Hardtack—a flour and water biscuit labeled "worm castles" by Concord's soldiers—in combination with coffee became daily staples, and the acute lack of fresh fruit and vegetables led to frequent cases of scurvy. While stealing from civilians was prohibited by regulation, when troops were traveling over difficult Southern terrain and far from supply depots, brigade commanders would order foraging parties, sometimes staffed by "bummers," shabby ruffians who would raid private dwellings and farms, stealing livestock, meat, corn, vegetables and whatever else was needed to maintain an army on the march.

Marching toward Fredericksburg, fully equipped Union regiments would have had little reason to think that this confrontation with Rebels would produce the most lopsided casualty figures of any engagement of the Civil War. Led by Army of the Potomac commander Major General Ambrose Burnside, U.S. losses were truly horrific, with almost 1,300 killed, close to 10,000 wounded and about 1,800 missing—either dead or captured. Robert E. Lee's forces suffered fewer than 5,400 killed and wounded. U.S. units and the Army of Virginia fielded the largest armies fought on a battlefield, with a total of 200,000 men at arms. Among the 106,000 soldiers under Burnside, there were close to 120 Concord soldiers representing thirteen Massachusetts regiments.

Those Massachusetts regiments included the 1st Massachusetts Volunteers, with six Concord men, one of whom, Thomas Drawbridge, is buried in Sleepy Hollow. Private Martin Lynch was in Company E, 9th Massachusetts, and died of wounds suffered at Fredericksburg on December 31, twenty days following the battle. The 11th Massachusetts included ten foot soldiers from Concord, with Patrick Holland becoming a POW at a later date and dying at Andersonville, Georgia. The 13th Regiment enrolled seven from Concord, with three of its members deserting in 1863–64. Private John Lupicelle, a member of the 15th, deserted his regiment eight months following Fredericksburg. (Desertion will be a topic treated later.) The 19th Massachusetts, with four Concord soldiers involved, was loaded into small boats during a Union plan developed by engineers to move their pontoons up close to the river in a bridge-building operation at the Rappahannock. However, with Lee occupying the high ground, Burnside's legions were battered, and he ordered a re-cross, pulling up the bridges behind him.

The 32nd Massachusetts, commanded by Lieutenant Colonel George Prescott, had forty-three Concord men on the rolls, any number of whom were wounded or killed in engagements from 1863 to 1865. Of course, Prescott fell mortally wounded on the battlefield near Petersburg in 1864. He was so highly regarded as a Concord hero that he was immortalized with these verses at his funeral service:

> *Deck out your old hills old Concord in all your summer pride,*
> *To welcome back your soldier who for liberty has died,*
> *Trail in the dust your weeping elms,*

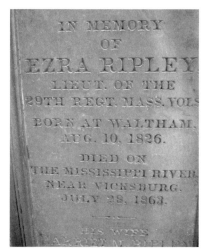

Lieutenant Ezra Ripley's grave. He died at Vicksburg. *Author's collection.*

And with pride and sorrow mingled,
prepare your dead to meet,
For he loved the gentle river, with its
calm and peaceful shore,
He loved the quiet village life, but he
loved the country more;
For he heard her earliest call for help,
and answering to the cry,
Showed how a soldier ought to fight,
and a Christian ought to die.

Remaining Massachusetts regiments at Fredericksburg included the "Fighting 20th," the 29th, the 35th, the 36th and the 1st Massachusetts Cavalry, with nine Concord cavalrymen. Within the 29th, First Lieutenant Ezra Ripley "sickened and died" in sultry heat around Vicksburg, Mississippi. Ripley, grandson and namesake of longtime Concord First Parish minister Ezra Ripley and a Harvard grad, had engaged in heavy fighting before Richmond and Antietam. A portion of his epitaph is copied here:

Of the best Pilgrim stock,
Descended from officers in the Revolutionary army
And from a long line of ministers of Concord,
He was worthy of his lineage.
An able and successful lawyer,
He gave himself with persistent zeal
to the cause of the friendless and the oppressed.
Of slender physical strength
and of a nature refined and delicate.
He was led by patriotism and the love of freedom
to leave home and friends for the toilsome labors of war,
and shrank from no fatigue and danger,
until worn out in her service,
He gave his life for his country.

Note: The last seven lines in this tribute to Ripley appear on his Grand Army of the Republic marker placed at his grave in Sleepy Hollow.

Chapter 6

1863

Road to Gettysburg

The 54th was mustered into service in March 1863 with Private George W. Dugan in its ranks, identified as "the only native colored man who went to the Civil War from *Concord*." Dugan, son of Thomas and Jennie Dugan of Concord, enlisted on February 20, 1863, and was registered on the rolls as age forty-four, a farmer and widower. His father, Thomas, was the third slave behind John Jack and Brister Freeman to own farmland in Concord, with his property near Old Marlboro Road. Thomas's wife, Jennie Dugan, who may have been born in Africa, arrived in Concord from Acton and made her own imprint. (Concord's Jennie Dugan Road runs off Old Marlboro Road.)

On January 26, Governor Andrew received Lincoln's imprimatur to form the 54th as the first regiment in the Union army composed of African American soldiers, although commanded by white officers. Up to that moment, there had been a solid wall of resistance to recruiting black men in the military service. In his 1863 report, the commonwealth's adjutant-general heaped praise on the governor for his astute foresight: "In the Executive of Massachusetts was found a man who could…stem these currents and carry out…the experiment of recruiting regiments of colored men." The governor was able to generate even greater interest in this newly formed unit by reaching out to the scion of a prominent Beacon Hill family, Robert Gould Shaw, to command the 54th with the designated rank of colonel. The saga of the 54th and Robert Gould Shaw was immortalized in the Augustus Saint Gaudens memorial on Boston Common, as well as the film *Glory*.

Private Dugan and the 54th, with strong abolitionist support, trained at Camp Meigs in Readville, and six weeks following his enlistment, the regiment was back in Boston, preparing for departure to South Carolina. Hundreds of cheering enthusiasts lined Boylston Street as columns of troops began their march. Wendell Phillips, William Lloyd Garrison, Governor Andrew and Frederick Douglass were all in attendance. Douglass, with two sons in the 54th, was stirred by the sight of Colonel Shaw riding at the head of the regiment proceeding down Beacon Street and entering Boston Common via the Charles Street gate. Douglass aroused the audience with these words: "Massachusetts was the first in the War of Independence; first to break the chain of slaves; first to make the black man equal before the law; first to admit colored children in her common schools; she was first to answer with her blood the alarm cry of the nation when its capital was menaced by the rebels." Reflecting on this dramatic moment for black soldiers, he uttered these noble words, "The iron gate of our prison stands half open, one gallant rush will fling it wide."

Marching from the Common to State Street, while hearing thunderous applause and the sounds of a brass and drum band, the unit made its way to Battery Wharf waiting to board the transport ship. The "gallant rush" with pluck and courage would not occur too soon, as initially the 54th was slated to provide ancillary support, principally manual labor. The unit's first battlefield action took place in July when the 54th engaged Confederate forces on James Island, South Carolina, losing 42 men in the confrontation. A few days later, 600 members of the 54th waited for the signal to attack the Confederate stronghold of Fort Wagner. With the white flag of Massachusetts held high, men under Shaw's command followed him to the top of the impregnable fort, thrust into hand-to-hand combat with the enemy. The slaughter resulted in 272 of the 600 troops in the 54th killed, wounded or captured, with Shaw among the fallen. Concord's Private George W. Dugan, Company A, the "only native colored man who went to the Civil War from this town," was killed in action and buried in the Atlantic sand with other fallen comrades. In this "gallant rush," Shaw may have thought of his 600 as comparable to Tennyson's Light Brigade:

> *Cannon to the right of them,*
> *Cannon to the left,*
> *Volleyed and thundered;*
> *Stormed at with shot and shell,*
> *Boldly they marched and well,*

Into the jaws of death,
Into the mouth of hell
Rode the Six Hundred.

Ralph Waldo Emerson was so moved by the death of Colonel Robert Gould Shaw that he wrote an epitaph that may well be applied to all Union army soldiers, most particularly our Concord men:

So near is God to man
When duty whispers low,
Thou must
The youth replies
I can

Governor John Andrew provided his own tribute to those Massachusetts men who engage in heroic deeds:

From the din of the battle they have passed to the peace of eternity. Farewell warrior, citizen, patriot, lover, friend; whether in the humbler ranks, or bearing the sword of official power, whether private, captain, surgeon or chaplain, for all these in the heady fight who passed away, Hail and Farewell.

The Massachusetts 54th, with George Dugan in the ranks, became pacesetters for 180,000 black soldiers to follow, filling 10 percent of the total Union army, 17 of whom received the Medal of Honor. In April 1864, the U.S. Congress passed an order declaring that black soldiers were equal to whites and referred to the meritorious service of the 54th. Lincoln paid his own tribute by declaring that the 180,000 black troops tipped the balance in the war.

Four Concord military officers were attached to African American units, including the 6th, 37th, 75th and 118th United States Colored Troops. Colonel John Ames was with the 6th; Captain Daniel Foster was regimental chaplain in the 37th; Captain George Buttrick served in the 75th; and Lieutenant George Willis, with prior service in the 1st Massachusetts, volunteered for the 118th. George Buttrick was the great-grandson of the Minutemen's Major John Buttrick and resided at the homestead on Liberty Street. All of these white officers, who were carefully chosen to lead these units, commended the black soldiers who served under them and recognized their contributions to the Union victory. When these units marched into Virginia with colors flying and bands playing, they were quite a sight. Sergeant John Broke described his experience passing through Fairfax Court: "The inhabitants looked at us with astonishment, as if we were some great monsters risen up out of the ground. They looked bewildered, yet it seemed to be too true and apparent to them that they really beheld nearly 10,000 colored soldiers filing by, armed to the teeth, with bayonets bristling in the sun—and I tell you our boys seemed to fully appreciate the importance of marching through a secesh town."[15]

CHANCELLORSVILLE

With the 54th preparing for South Carolina, 115,000 Union troops under General Joe Hooker were poised to engage 60,000 of Lee's finest, ten miles west of Fredericksburg, at the Battle of Chancellorsville. Hooker took up residence at Chancellor House, a Southern-styled mansion around which Hooker concentrated his army after the first day of fighting. Among those serving under Hooker was Brigadier General Amiel Weeks Whipple, who had graduated from West Point in 1841 and, twenty years later, three months before the outbreak of the war, became a brevet lieutenant colonel in the U.S. Army. In December 1862, he rose to brevet colonel as a result of gallant and meritorious service at Fredericksburg. Whipple's father had managed the Whipple Tavern, located close to Lee's Bridge on the Fitchburg Turnpike. The tavern, a former stagecoach stop, still stands on the east side of Nine Acre Corner and is part of the Wheeler Farm. Whipple attended the district school at Nine Acre Corner and then Amherst College prior to receiving an appointment to West Point upon the recommendation of the Honorable Samuel Hoar.

Chancellorsville was another setback for the Army of the Potomac, as Lee outmaneuvered Hooker by splitting his outnumbered force and halting the Federal advance. It proved to be a costly victory for the Confederates as Lee's casualties numbered thirteen thousand, prominent among them Stonewall Jackson, who was shot by his own pickets and died as a result of developing pneumonia following amputation of his left arm. On the Union side, General Whipple was severely wounded during the battle and died three days later on May 7, 1862. Abraham Lincoln had established a friendship with Whipple when the then brigadier general was headquartered at Arlington House, the former Lee estate, while commanding forces protecting Washington.

As a result of this association, Lincoln not only attended his friend's funeral but was also instrumental in the naming of a military installation Fort Whipple in memory of posthumously promoted Major General Amiel Whipple. Fort Whipple would later become Fort Myer, home to the 3rd U.S. Infantry Regiment, known as the "Old Guard." It serves as escort to the president and provides full military honors at Arlington National Cemetery and the Tomb of the Unknown Soldier. On May 13, 1862, President Lincoln wrote a letter to the superintendent of West Point, recommending the appointment of Whipple's son, William, to the military academy. In 2010, members of a prominent Concord family petitioned the town to operate a bed-and-breakfast at 148/154 Fitchburg Turnpike. In their appeal, they referenced the history of this Whipple Tavern as a stagecoach stop and described the longtime cultivated Lee/Wheeler/ Brigham farmland in that area.

While Concord men were defining the combat story of a war that was grinding on with neither side gaining an advantage, townspeople continued to live their lives while following the campaigns in the South. In the aftermath of Lincoln's 1863 Emancipation Proclamation, Ralph Waldo Emerson wrote the "Boston Hymn" in praise of the president. Initially, Emerson had been deeply conflicted by the coming of the Civil War, but he now began to see it as a "cleansing fire" that would result in God, in the person of Lincoln, breaking the bonds of slavery. His hymn was read at the Boston Music Hall and later to a private audience that included Louisa May Alcott, Bronson Alcott and Julia Ward Howe, who read her own "Battle Hymn." Emerson's words rang resoundingly:

> *I break your bonds and masterships,*
> *And I unchain the slave:*
> *Free be his heart and hand henceforth,*
> *As wind and wandering wave.*

The Concord Town Report made mention of changes in the draft law in 1863, with much stricter provisions that called for all male citizens twenty to thirty-five and all unmarried men thirty-five to forty-five to be subject to military duty. Federal officials entered all eligible men into a lottery, but you could avoid service by hiring a substitute or by paying the government $300 to be classified exempt. Among those paying the $300 fee were future president Grover Cleveland and John D. Rockefeller. In many ways, this war was accurately labeled "a poor man's fight." Beyond these legal escape clauses, more than 160,000 men in the North refused to report to their draft boards for examination. By way of comparison, Concord's record was commendable. In March 1863, the draft required 26 men from Concord, and 23 were furnished, which was considered "a better result than any of the other 43 sub-districts, except two."

While Concord officialdom continued to follow Concord soldiers' progress on the battlefield during the third year of the war, local matters commanded attention as well. The 1863–64 Town Report highlighted the need for a new high school house to replace the existing structure located on Sudbury Road, which was directly behind the present library. Town selectmen and the School Committee summarized the need for enlargement by stating that the current school "is crowded into the smallest and most inconvenient of school rooms...the town needs a new school suited to the demands of the times. It should be two stories high with two schoolrooms and ample grounds. The question of high school accommodations is to be submitted fresh to you at our town meeting." At the town meeting the following April, there was an affirmative vote to build a new high school house, expenses not to exceed $10,000. The existing schoolhouse would be sold to E.R. Hoar.

Beyond the request for a new school, the committee solicited parental support: "No doubt many a father or mother says: How can I help the schools, I have little or no time to visit them? They can more and more thoroughly believe in education...take a more practical interest in the subject of education." The extensive daily curriculum for the high school was outlined as follows:

> *Two classes in French*
> *Three in Latin*
> *One on Book-Keeping*
> *One in Surveying*
> *One in Natural Philosophy*
> *One in German*
> *One in Greek*
> *One in Geometry*
> *One in Astronomy*
> *Exercises in Reading, Elocution and English Composition*

Other budgetary line items in the Town Report included:

Nathan B. Stow's services as Selectman: $20.00
Nathan Barrett's services on School Committee: $7.50
Paid to Moses Hobson—$1.12 for repairs to high school
Dr. H.A. Barrett, expenses to Gettysburg: $52.50 [perhaps for surgical
work following the three-day battle in July]
Town of Lincoln reimbursement of money received for Civil War recruits
[enlistment bonus money?]
*Committee of Sleepy Hollow Cemetery: four new paths laid out, with Mr.
James having done most of the work on the grounds at $1.50 per day*

A permanent private fund was established for the support of the cemetery
with $1,025 raised to date for this "beautiful home of the dead." There were
thirty-nine deaths in 1863, with one soldier among them. This may have
been Private Charles Brigham, who died on February 15 and was buried at
Sleepy Hollow.

Desertion in the Ranks

Beyond Concord's yearly report, Governor Andrew addressed wartime
matters in his 1863 address to the state legislature. Referencing troop
requirements for the year, the governor emphasized his insistence that
every corps should receive a full outfit and equipment before leaving the
commonwealth and went on to express his thanks for the assistance he
received from municipal authorities across the state. Andrew recommended
that bounties paid to enlistees should be equalized statewide and be
reimbursed by Massachusetts property and polls tax dollars. He also referred
to the cases of deserters, which he said were rare, suggesting that only a small
number of men had "manifestly deserted." However, records maintained by
both sides in the Civil War suggest that both the Army of the Potomac and
the Army of Virginia were plagued by desertions. Union deserters ranged
between 9 and 12 percent, while attrition among Virginians was between 10
and 15 percent.

In compiling numbers, it was important to distinguish "stragglers" from
"deserters," recognizing that some soldiers went AWOL for a brief period
with every intention of returning to the ranks, while others fled permanently.

"Stragglers" were those who left and returned, while "deserters" were absent for more than thirty days without returning to their companies.

Union army deserters totaled well over 200,000 during the life of the war, with 8,726 recorded in Massachusetts, a 7.37 percent desertion rate, placing the state eleventh in the Union. By way of comparison, New York listed 44,913 deserters, with 24,050 in Pennsylvania and 18,354 in Ohio. In Concord, out of 450 town enlistees from 1861 to 1865, 13 deserted and 1 soldier was dishonorably discharged. Concord's George Tobin and Frank Stewart, both serving in the 12th Massachusetts Volunteers, deserted on the same day, August 18, 1863, and one of their fellow Concord soldiers, Frederick Morris, went AWOL three days later. Three months later, Private Peter Daley deserted from Company G.

What were the contributing factors that prompted Union army desertions at such a rate? The daily hardship of war exacted a heavy toll, with war-weary soldiers serving in units with high regimental casualty rates from battle wounds and disease. Beyond battle fatigue, a common denominator for unauthorized absences, the less able soldier struggled with forced marches, strict military discipline, tedious monotony, illness, thirst, hunger, acute family needs at home, lowered morale, delay in pay, lack of respect for commanding officers and discouragement with military setbacks. During the first six months of trying to adapt to the rigors of war, a soldier was particularly vulnerable to contracting a serious disease or illness. Reviewing three Concord deserters from the 12th Massachusetts, Tobin, Stewart and Morris, all of whom abandoned the field in August 1863, their regiment engaged in some of the heaviest fighting of the war. They fought at Second Bull Run in August 1862, followed by significant regimental losses at Antietam a month later, with substantial casualties at Fredericksburg in December. In 1863, this regiment participated in the Battle of Chancellorsville in May and subsequently performed valuable service with severe losses at Gettysburg. It was a war-torn regiment coming out of these engagements, which may account for four Concord soldiers deserting their companies by November 1863.

Southern records identified 104,000 Confederate deserters, enough of a concern for military commanders that they requested the adoption of strict measures to prevent further attrition. In the June 30, 1863 edition of the *Staunton (VA) Spectator*, Colonel Harmon of the 52nd Regiment asked citizens of the valley to provide socks for his troops and further "requests information on all members of the regiment who are home without leave." A later issue of this publication scolds the Army of Virginia for its lack of discipline and organization, "so defective that those already in the army are permitted to desert in such numbers as to dangerously diminish its strength."

It went on to lament the lawless violence committed by deserters that placed life and property in danger. Some months earlier, Stonewall Jackson ordered three men shot in front of open graves while thousands witnessed the executions. About five hundred men, North and South, were shot or hanged, two-thirds of them for desertion. Indeed, the War Department in Washington, adjacent to the White House, issued General Orders announcing that "those convicted of desertion were to be shot to death with musketry, at such time and such place as the commanding general may direct." Within the Executive Mansion, President Lincoln often exercised his pardon authority in foregoing executing a soldier, suggesting that he too might "skedaddle" if he were in the same situation. More importantly, Lincoln was reluctant to expand the carnage of this war by encouraging the use of firing squads, unless extreme circumstances warranted it.

Chapter 7

THE GETTYSBURG FRONT

From another battlefield, following a deadly artillery strike that vaporized thirty-three of his comrades, a U.S. Army captain wrote, "The limitations of life come into sharp relief; no one is indispensable in this world."[16] These words could describe three horrific days in July 1863 that made a small town in Pennsylvania historical and unforgettable in the annals of warfare.

The largest battle in the Western Hemisphere brought 165,000 soldiers into Gettysburg, towing 530 cannons that would fire fifty thousand artillery shells. Additionally, some 250 tons of musket and rifle ammunition were expended, including 7 million rounds of ammunition—a colossal total until you consider that it required one hundred rifle or revolver shots to inflict a single casualty. In *The Republic of Suffering*, Drew Faust recorded 6 million pounds of human and animal carcasses over the course of the three-day battle, with 22,000 wounded left behind for a town of 2,400 citizens to grapple with. Union casualties totaled 23,049, with 28,000 dead, wounded and missing in Lee's Army, exacting a cost on a scale that is almost incomprehensible. When Lee retreated during the night of July 3, he left his dead for the town to bury and thousands of wounded to care for. With the wounded at ten times the population of the town, and few doctors and support personnel left behind, the medical and burial tasks were formidable. With temperatures in the upper eighties and sweltering humidity, the putrid odors created a lingering smell of death that lasted for months, so potent that residents carried peppermint oil in an attempt to neutralize the stench. Fearing disease from decaying flesh, disinfectant and hundreds of bags of lime were spread on the roads.

"When the smoke cleared," there were six Concord soldiers among the casualties, three dead and the same number wounded. Private Francis ("Frank") Buttrick of the 32nd Massachusetts Volunteers died on July 28 from wounds received during the second day of fighting, an account of which is described by George Gray, a fellow Concord soldier serving in the 20th Massachusetts Volunteer Infantry. Writing in "Memories of Concord Veterans of the Civil War," Gray chronicled the aftermath of the Battle of Gettysburg while he was transporting all medical supplies belonging to the brigade. As his medical wagon neared Gettysburg, he began to encounter the wounded, including Major General Daniel Sickles, whose tactical error on day two of the battle nearly resulted in a major Union defeat. Sickles had violated orders by pushing his troops forward of a defensive line, creating a gap in a fishhook perimeter. Struck in the right leg by a twelve-pound shot and removed from the battlefield, Sickles underwent a thigh amputation, prompting one soldier in blue to comment that "it was a bad day for Sickles but a good day for the Union Army." The major general's leg was transported to a museum, complete with a card that read "with the compliments of M.G. D.E. Sickles." It now resides at the National Museum of Health and Medicine in Silver Springs, Maryland. (This author viewed it in its prior home at Walter Reed Army Hospital.)

In the company of Sickles's stretcher bearers, Gray traveled two miles to the field hospital and reported to the surgeon, who was pleased to see him arrive with badly needed medical supplies. Gray then described the next event:

> *We soon got into working order, dressing wounds, when the word came to move. The Confederates had concentrated their batteries where Pickett was about to make his terrific charge at 1PM, when they shelled us, with missiles falling where we were located. We had to get out of there in a hurry. We had several wounded there, but they were removed in safety. Among them, the colonel of the 20th Massachusetts, Colonel Paul Revere of Boston, descendent of Paul Revere of Revolutionary War fame and brother of Assistant Surgeon Revere who was killed at Antietam. Colonel Revere was wounded in the lungs and died that night. The wounded were left in our hands; we had no building of any kind and no tents for a day or two, but soon tents arrived. It was here that there were more amputations performed than any other place I had seen. Perhaps you will say I exaggerate when I say I have seen more than one pile*

of limbs here that would fill a common horse cart.

The weather being warm, there was not air enough. The surgeon had many of the trees cut down, and that let the sun in to such an extent it created such a sickening odor by so much blood and the close quarters of so many wounded that we were obliged to move again, for the third time, to open ground where they could receive better and more air. Of course, we had many deaths. It was here that young Frank Buttrick of this town died of wounds. [Private Frank

Francis Buttrick's grave. He died from wounds at Gettysburg. *Author's collection.*

Buttrick of Company B, 32nd Massachusetts, was twenty-one and a Concord farmer when he enlisted on November 28, 1863. Wounded on July 2, he died on August 6.]

One day a stranger came in search of a young man by the name of Buttrick that had been wounded. I showed him where he lay. He said he had come to take him home. I told him he could not be moved then and probably would not live but a short time. He then introduced himself as Samuel Staples of Concord. I invited him to remain as my guest and he accepted. Young Buttrick died the next day. Mr. Staples was able to start for home, taking Buttrick with him, that he might be laid at rest amongst his friends, and where his grave can be strewn with flowers by his friends of boyhood days and by his comrades in arms.

Gray remained at Gettysburg for six weeks and then broke camp and prepared to start for Virginia again. Sheriff Sam Staples, who claimed Buttrick's body, was the Concord constable who arrested Thoreau in 1846 for failure to pay his poll tax. Stopping Thoreau while en route to the cobbler's shop, coming from his cabin at Walden Pond, Staples offered to pay Thoreau's tax for him, but when Thoreau refused on principle to accept Staples's offer, he was jailed. Staples must have been very resourceful in locating Buttrick, for hundreds of thousands of dead soldiers were unidentified on the battlefield, leaving families with no knowledge of how loved ones died or where they might be interred. Soldiers did not wear dog tags, and there was no Federal system in place to notify next of kin or assist families in "repatriating" deceased soldiers.

Francis ("Frank") Channing Barlow lived in the house at the corner of Court Lane and Bedford Street, property now owned by the Dee family, two doors up from their funeral home behind the Town House. Barlow became the only Concord-connected soldier who enlisted as a private and rose to the rank of major general. Born in Brooklyn, New York, in 1834, where his father served as pastor of the Unitarian Church, young Frank and his mother, Amelia, were abandoned by Reverend Barlow, who was by then deeply mired in liquor. Relocating to the Concord area, Amelia became enamored of the neighboring utopian commune, Brook Farm, which brought her into contact with Hawthorne, Emerson and other Concord luminaries who sought to establish a gentle life at this experimental farm community. Frank thoroughly enjoyed interacting with Emerson, Ebenezer Hoar and other prominent members of this intellectual circle, all of whom devoted extended time to discussing issues of the day. This was solid training for a Harvard education that led to a successful law practice in New York City, where he prospered while indulging in New York's societal life.

One day after marrying Arabella Griffith on April 20, 1861, Barlow went to war, ultimately transitioning from a kind, contemplative member of New York society to a toughened combat general leading troops at Antietam, where he was severely wounded, and at Gettysburg, where he was badly wounded again, only to return to the front for the Wilderness campaign in 1864. It's a remarkable story for a commanding Civil War figure and his loving wife, and it began with Lieutenant Barlow's assignment to the 12th New York Volunteer Militia; subsequently deployed to Washington to defend the capital, he was later dispatched to Harper's Ferry. Arabella accompanied her husband throughout his military campaigns and became a Civil War nurse attached to the Sanitary Commission in 1862; she tended to her husband after he was inflicted with several wounds, as well as treated other wounded Union soldiers following Chancellorsville and Gettysburg.

Following the end of his three-month enlistment, Frank joined the 61st New York Volunteers; now with the rank of colonel, he served under General George McClellan in the Maryland campaign. Later on, a group photo taken by Mathew Brady reveals a dashing figure posing with General

Winfield Scott Hancock and two other division commanders. Leaning against a tree, Brigadier General Frank Barlow stands out in his uniform jacket, complete with a black-and-white checkered shirt, a white collar, a black bow tie, a leather belt with silver buckle and a ceremonial sword with leather torso strap. While the photo is not dated, Barlow was promoted to brigadier general on September 19, 1862, two days after the Battle of Antietam. While his battlefield performance may have justified his new rank, his promotion was assisted by written endorsements from Ralph Waldo Emerson, Nathaniel Hawthorne and Oliver Wendell Holmes.

Wounded at Antietam but with Arabella at his side, Barlow was nursed back to health in time to rejoin his regiment for the Battle of Gettysburg, where he was hit on the left side by a shell that exploded over his head when his unit was overwhelmed by General Jubal Early's Confederate forces. Severely wounded and not removed from the battlefield by his comrades, he was transported by Confederates to the Josiah Benner farmhouse on Old Harrisburg Road. (This property was obtained by Gettysburg National Military Park in 2001.) He was not expected to survive but was treated by two women and then exchanged by Early's troops.

Once again, Arabella tended to her husband, and following a period of convalescence, Frank returned to the trenches for the Wilderness campaign in the spring of 1864. On August 1, he was promoted to brevet major general for "meritorious conduct throughout the campaign." In all of these significant military engagements, Arabella was devoted to her duties, valiantly carrying on despite becoming ill following the Petersburg campaign. Her illness developed into typhoid fever, which took her life several weeks later, leaving Frank distraught. Taking a leave of absence following his wife's death, Frank returned home in March 1865 and later resigned from the Army of the Potomac, only to rejoin on April 6, three days before Lee's surrender.

The harsh reality of this war was a recognition that civilians perished from the same diseases that caused military casualties and that prominent families were stricken by the same war-borne illnesses. Frank Barlow lost his beloved Arabella; Lincoln lost his eleven-year-old son, Willie, to typhoid; Confederate general James Longstreet lost two children to scarlet fever; Union general William T. Sherman's young son died of typhoid; and Louisa May Alcott was inflicted with the same insidious disease. While battlefields were upholstered with dead bodies, contagions and epidemics produced the preponderance of civilian and military deaths.

One of the few men in the Civil War who would rise from enlisted private to general, Major General Francis Barlow was invited back to Concord to become chief marshal of the 1875 Concord Centennial, leading the procession to the North Bridge, where President Ulysses S. Grant presided at the dedication of Daniel Chester French's minuteman statue. Barlow died in 1896, but in 1922, an eight-and-a-half-foot-tall bronze monument of General Francis Channing Barlow appeared on the battlefield at Gettysburg National Military Park in tribute to his distinguished service to the Union. Barlow's monument is one of 1,324 monuments, markers, statues and plaques on six thousand acres of this battlefield. In words spoken at the dedication of the monument to his 20th Maine regiment, Joshua Lawrence Chamberlain, hero of Little Round Top, summarized Gettysburg's battlefield heroics in glowing terms: "In great deeds something abides. On great fields something stays. Forms change and pass; bodies disappear, but spirits linger."

In addition to Private Francis Buttrick and Brigadier General Francis Barlow, other Concord casualties in the Battle of Gettysburg included Colonel George Prescott, previously described as wounded in the Wheatfield; First Sergeant Charles Bowers, also wounded; and Private Barney Clark and First Sergeant Charles Appleton, both of whom died from their wounds. Appleton, serving with the 32nd Massachusetts, was killed on the first day of the battle and was buried by the side of the road between Gettysburg and Taneytown, leaving behind a young wife and two children. Three Concord dead and three Concord wounded were the town's costs in this cornerstone battle of the Civil War.

Recalling Private Herman Flint, the first Concord man to die in Union army service and buried at Suffolk, Virginia, his brother, Rockwood, mustered in for three years of service in the fall of 1861, five days before his sixteenth birthday. Born on November 9, 1845, on the east side of the North Road (Monument Street) just across from the Concord River, Rockwood and Herman were descendants of Thomas Flint, one of the first and certainly most influential Concord settlers. This highly motivated boy of fifteen was "anxious to go" to war, and in his memoirs, recorded in "Memories of Concord Veterans of the Civil War," he described his walk to the Town House to enlist: "I found that the enlistment roll lay on a table at the head of the winding stairs leading up into our Town Hall—I mustered up enough courage to go and sign my name."

Seven months into his military service, he came down with typhoid fever and was dispatched to a hospital in Washington for treatment on the same day his brother died in camp in Suffolk, Virginia. Rockwood wrote that Herman's death was attributable to "bathing when over-heated. He was the first man that Concord lost in the war…I came pretty near being the same once." Herman Flint's name is the eleventh name listed on the soldiers' monument, not one hundred feet from the steps of the Town House, where he and his brother affixed their names to the enlistment rolls.

Serving in the 32nd Massachusetts Volunteers, Rockwood provided a detailed account of an army on the move; he subsisted on green corn and potatoes pillaged from neighboring fields. During periods when the army was "reduced almost to starvation, it could not be prevented, despite strict orders regarding foraging." In July 1862, after "constantly marching and halting, halting and marching, often at night," the 32nd met the enemy at Gettysburg and at "Devil's Den," a deep hollow in the regiment's front. Flint described the latter engagement: "We were hardly in position here before the attack came again and the battle grew hot and furious. We had been engaged but a short period of time when Colonel Prescott was struck and carried from the field." There were 81 killed or wounded out of the 227 whom the 32nd took into the fight at Gettysburg.

A month later, at Beverly Ford, Rockwood Flint witnessed the execution of five deserters, "all of whom were dressed alike in white shirts, trousers, shoes and caps. With the band playing the death march, the five doomed men marched across the field to their graves where each was seated upon his coffin. Eighty men selected from the provost guard were posted to fire the fatal volley—forty loaded with blank and forty with ball cartridges were discharged—and all was over." Wounded on May 12, 1864, Rockwood Flint mustered out on November 4, 1864, and returned to Concord, where he resumed work as a carpenter and builder.

Massachusetts was well represented at Gettysburg, with eighteen infantry regiments, combined with four heavy artillery batteries and one cavalry regiment, for a combined total of twenty-three regiments engaged in the field of fire. At least fifty-six Concord soldiers fought at Gettysburg, serving in the 1st, 15th, 19th, 20th and 22nd Infantry Regiments, along with the 1st Regiment of Cavalry and the 1st Regiment Volunteer Heavy Artillery, which included Concord's three Melvin brothers—Privates Asa, John and Samuel—all of whom were destined for distinction as fallen warriors. In reliving his own military experience with the 20th Massachusetts, Oliver Wendell Holmes reminded his fellow veterans that they "shared the incommunicable experience of war." The Melvin brothers shared the gallant sacrifice of that war.

John Shepard Keyes, having served as a bodyguard at Lincoln's inauguration in 1860, following which he was appointed a U.S. marshal by the president, now accompanied Lincoln to Gettysburg on November

18, 1863, the same year in which Keyes bought the Bullet Hole House on Monument Street as a gift for his wife, Martha. Lincoln had been invited to make "a few appropriate remarks" at the consecration of the Gettysburg National Cemetery, a campaign that began with the reburial of Union soldiers in October, three months after the battle. Keyes's connection with Lincoln had come a long way since he first laid eyes on him, when Lincoln was president-elect and Keyes was in New York City. Witnessing Lincoln riding in an open carriage, Keyes wrote in his autobiography that he "thought him the homeliest man I had ever set eyes on. I wrote home that he was a cross between Jake Farmer and Beauty Wetherbee, the two homeliest farmers in Concord."[17] Now, almost three years later, Keyes described Lincoln's presence in Gettysburg as "the supreme moment of the war," as Lincoln, his cabinet and other dignitaries arrived at the cemetery under escort of U.S. troops, with periodic rain showers threatening the processional. Keyes and Lincoln, in words transcribed by the Concord Free Public Library, were struck by the "piles of shot marks of bullet, rusted bayonets and equipment, dead horses and splintered gun carriages"; here they were witnessing the scene of carnage more than four months after the battle.

Tall in the saddle, the president's mounted bodyguard wrote that he valued Lincoln's "few immortal sentences that will always be his best words." Keyes may have agreed with a spectator, who referenced the president's high-pitched voice that had a thin quality yet carried well and was heard quite distinctly by the crowd. Born in Kentucky, Lincoln's voice had an intonation that resulted in a long *o*, so that the audience heard him say he was "dedicated *toe* the proposition" and, "We have come *toe* dedicate a portion of that field." Yet his most profound theme resonated clearly, when he expressed the hope that those who died at Gettysburg "shall not have died in vain—that this nation under God, shall have a new birth of freedom."

The Siege of Vicksburg

On the night of July 2, 1863, President Lincoln anxiously paced back and forth in the telegraph office at the War Department, located on mansion grounds on the west side of the White House. With pivotal engagements about to begin in both Gettysburg and Vicksburg, Lincoln was desperate for word from Meade in Pennsylvania and Grant in Tennessee. A Confederate defeat in Gettysburg would stop Lee's march north, and after thirteen months of fighting along the Mississippi River, Lincoln knew that control of this area was the key to an ultimate Union victory. Vicksburg was a thriving river port before the war, and the bluffs above the city provided a strategic advantage, with capabilities of unleashing cannon fire on Union gunboats below.

In late May, following a massive amphibious operation with significant land forces, Grant's troops dug in at Vicksburg, and for six weeks, Union artillery shelled the city, blasting Rebel trenches as well as civilian caves that had been dug out of the bluffs in response to intense cannon fire. Finally, on July 4, the day after Lee's defeat in Gettysburg, Vicksburg fell into Union hands. While Grant's victory was costly, exacting ten thousand casualties, Confederate losses numbered the same, not including thirty thousand Rebel soldiers forced to surrender. In addition, Union forces recovered 172 Confederate cannons and sixty thousand rifled muskets. Overshadowed by Gettysburg, the contemporaneous victory at Vicksburg delivered a solid one-two punch to Confederate forces. Vicksburg was an early indicator of Grant's willingness to sustain horrific losses in the interest of winning the war quickly by overwhelming the enemy with brute force. He attacked like a pit bull, mounting rapid thrusts, even knowing that with twice the number of troops you can outlast your adversary. This strategy was very consistent with Lincoln's view of warfare. It's not enough to carry the day by pushing the enemy off the battlefield. The only way to win the war is to defeat Lee's army.

With the raising of the white flag at Vicksburg, thousands paraded to the White House. Led by the band of the 34th Massachusetts Volunteers, they serenaded the president at the White House and then proceeded to Secretary of War Stanton's home on K Street, followed by a procession to Secretary of State Seward's residence at Lafayette Square, directly across from the Executive Mansion.

Among the casualties in the Mississippi siege was Concord's First Lieutenant Ezra Ripley, who while serving in the 39th Massachusetts died on July 28 at Vicksburg. Ezra was the grandson of Reverend Ezra Ripley (1751–1841), minister of Concord's First Parish for almost sixty-three years, and his paternal grandmother was also the grandmother of Ralph Waldo Emerson, making Ezra and Waldo stepgrandsons. The Ripleys lived in the Old Manse, adjacent to the North Bridge on Monument Street, a site that included land donated by Reverend Ripley for a proposed monument to be dedicated in 1835 in celebration of the town's bicentennial.

Ezra, son of noted transcendentalist Sarah Alden Bradford Ripley and Samuel Ripley, minister of First Parish in Waltham, enlisted as a first lieutenant in Company B, 29th Infantry, at the age of thirty-five on July 24, 1861, following ten years of legal work as an attorney in East Cambridge. In a Harvard memorial biography, he was referred to as "slender, delicate, sensitive and peculiarly unwarlike; not in robust health, but with steadfast enthusiasm set his face steadfastly to do what seemed to him to be his duty."[18] As evidence of his devotion to duty, in September 1862, following sick leave in Washington, and without money, Ezra hurried a long distance on foot to locate his regiment near Antietam, having spent one night sleeping on a haystack.

The official record of Lieutenant Ripley's death indicates that he "died of disease as a result of sultry heat" on July 28, 1863, in Vicksburg. His body had been left at Helena, Arkansas, but was later brought home to Concord and interred at Sleepy Hollow. Portions of his epitaph include the following: "Of the best Pilgrim stock…he was worthy of his lineage…he gave himself with persistent zeal to the cause of the friendless and the oppressed. He was led by patriotism and the love of freedom to leave home and friends for the toilsome labors of war, and shrank from no fatigue and danger, until worn out in her service, he gave his life for his country."

Traumatized by the death of her beloved son, the Civil War scarred Sarah's peaceful days in Concord, days that had been spent in the company of the Emersons, Alcotts, Franklin Sanborn, Channing and Hawthorne. This self-educated, brilliant woman—who tutored boys preparing for Harvard and raised seven children following the death of her husband in 1847—died in 1867 and was buried in the family plot across from the Emersons on Author's Ridge. Joan Goodwin, author of *The Remarkable Mrs. Ripley*, wrote of the oft-repeated legend of Sarah. It was said that she could simultaneously rock a cradle, shell peas, listen to one student recite his Latin and another his Greek.

Sarah Alden Bradford Ripley (1793–1867), descended from prominent Pilgrim families, is another one of these remarkable Concord women who filled the void in wartime by raising children, looking out for neighbors, running businesses, working in factories, managing farms, sewing flags and uniforms, serving as battlefield nurses and locating and caring for injured or dead soldiers. The entry of women into the workforce and nursing profession when men went off to war opened doors that had previously been closed and would set the stage for the suffrage movement later on.

The year 1863 closed with Private Frederick Pratt, who was drafted in July of that year, serving with the 1st Provincial Guard, with duty on Long Island and Boston Harbor, and in the "Soldiers and Sailors" report compiled in 1908, he is identified as "the only Concord man who was drafted and served, as far as known." While his service is commendable, Pratt is the only Concord soldier among 450 local soldiers, and some sailors, who did not voluntarily enlist to serve the Union.

Chapter 8

1864

The Melvin Brothers in the War

Peaceful [they] *sleep, with all our rights adorned*
Forever honored and forever mourned.
—*Homer,* Iliad

History remembers Gettysburg as a decisive moment in the Civil War, but while it was a bloody engagement, its role in the conflict needs to be placed in perspective. By the spring of 1864, Lee had recouped his losses, allowing the Army of Virginia to regain its fighting strength and continue the duel with Grant for another twenty-one months.

Meanwhile, early in 1864, Abraham Lincoln replied to 195 Concord schoolchildren, who with their teacher, Mary Rice, had petitioned the president to eliminate slavery. Mrs. Rice was a "station master" on the Underground Railroad, as well as a teacher at the Infant School in the Wright Tavern. In his letter to another Concord teacher, Mrs. Horace Mann, the president wrote, "Please tell these little people I am very glad their young hearts are so full of just and generous sympathy, and that while I have not the power to grant all they ask, I trust they will remember that God has, and that, as it seems, he wills to do it." (The original letter is archived at the Library of Congress.)

In the same month that Lincoln wrote his letter, the Town of Concord voted to build a new "high school house" with $10,000 appropriated to purchase the land and build the schoolhouse. In addition, the roof of the nine-year-old leaking Town House was repaired. An examination of receipts and expenses for the year revealed the following:

Receipts:
License of four dogs…$3.60
Poll tax of soldiers…$6.00 [the poll tax preserved the right of suffrage to soldiers and sailors, waiving previous missed payments for Concord men at war]
Town agent for sales of liquors…$264.06

Expenses:
Paid to William Brow…$1.25 for pail dipper and broom—District 4 schoolhouse
Darby brothers for school broom…65 cents
Paid A.C. Collier for winding clock [town clock at First Parish Church] *from August 1 1864 to March 1, 1865…$14.00*
At Sleepy Hollow, 800 young pines were set out on the slope or sandbank of the hill and a row of arbor vitae was set out in the spring between the two main gates on Bedford Street.

By the time these young pines were taking root in Sleepy Hollow, three Concord brothers—Asa, John and Samuel Melvin—all members of Company K, 1st Massachusetts Heavy Artillery, had died, either in battle, in a hospital or in a Confederate prison.

On April 19, 1861, Asa Melvin abandoned his labor on the Hiram Jones farm on Westford Road, where he had been employed for three years, and walked two and a half miles down Lowell Road to the center of town to salute the Concord Artillery as it was heading to war. This trek was the beginning of an odyssey that would lead to the last symbolic resting place of three brothers now embodied in a marble shrine as a sculpted reminder of man's love for country.

At twenty-seven, Asa was the oldest of the three brothers, but upon hearing that Captain George Prescott's roster was not full, he was the first of the Melvins to enlist; he left Concord with the company just three hours after responding to the call. A farmer by training, Asa began working for Hiram Jones following his father's death in August 1858. Hiram had married Mary Joanna Heald, and Asa's mother was Caroline Heald Melvin, so there was a family connection between Jones and the Melvins. With the Jones farm on Westford Road, the birthplace of the Melvin brothers was off Lowell Road, on the immediate north side of what is now Lindsay Pond Road. Ruth Wheeler, author of *Concord: Climate for Freedom*, described it as "the old wood house" built on the

Melvin farm. The house no longer stands, as it was burned to the ground by vandals in 1903.

Melvin's ancestors on his paternal side participated in King Philip's War, and one, Amos Melvin, played a key role at the outbreak of the American Revolution when he rang Concord's courthouse bell, rousing townspeople on April 19, 1775. On his mother's side, four of the Healds were officers serving in four distinct colonial companies. No wonder Asa, while not an initial member of the company, was quite willing to "leave the plow in the furrow" and march with the Concord Artillery. He was in the First Battle of Bull Run and, following meritorious service in that engagement, returned to Concord upon expiration of his one-hundred-day tour. Asa reenlisted in August 1862, this time in the 1st Massachusetts Heavy Artillery, and was killed (shot in the chest) just before the Battle of Petersburg and then interred in a mass grave in Spotsylvania, Virginia. At a reunion of the 1st Massachusetts Heavy Artillery, Colonel J. Payson Bradley referred to Asa as "a good soldier, spoken well of by all his comrades and officers." One of his former soldiers in Company K, Sylvester Frost, upon placing a wreath on Asa's tablet at the Melvin Memorial, said, "I deposit this wreath as a token of love and respect to the memory of our brave comrade, Asa H. Melvin of Company K."

John Melvin, second son of Asa Sr. and Caroline, enlisted in Company K at the age of twenty on July 5, 1861. Both John and his brother Samuel had been working at a textile mill in Lawrence prior to their enlistments. In October 1863, John was stricken with dysentery and succumbed to it at the Fort Albany Military Hospital in Virginia. His brother Asa kept a bedside vigil, and in conjunction with John's request, an army chaplain was present when he died. According to Samuel, John was treated with opium, but it "did no good." Having struggled all day on the thirteenth, he died peacefully at 11:00 p.m. Samuel packed John's personal belongings, sent seventy dollars of his back pay home and, honoring his brother's request, burned his letters. His body was routed to Concord and buried alongside his mother in the family plot at Sleepy Hollow—the only one of the three fallen brothers to be buried in that cemetery. With John Melvin's service to nation complete, Emerson's words at Sleepy Hollow speak to life's duty: "In this quiet valley, as in the palm of nature's hand, we shall sleep well when we have finished the day." John's company commander, Captain William H. Morrow, said of John that "he was an exceedingly good soldier. He was a man who kept his equipment and clothing in perfect shape at all times. No sudden call for any inspection ever found John Melvin unprepared."

In May 1864, just shy of the end of his three-year enlistment with the 1st Massachusetts, Sam Melvin was preparing to join the Army of the Potomac when he was captured at Harris Farm, Virginia, and sent south to Andersonville, where he was imprisoned at the military stockade at Camp Sumter. Built in early 1864, this prison was in operation for fourteen months, with forty-five thousand Union soldiers confined during that period.

Spread out over twenty-six and a half acres, the stockade was composed of hewed pine logs sixteen feet high with sentry boxes positioned at ninety-foot intervals. With four hundred inmates arriving daily, incarcerated in a makeshift facility with inadequate housing, food, clothing and medical care, the mortality rate was very high. Some thirteen thousand Union soldiers died at Sumter, Sam Melvin among them. He died at Andersonville on September 25, 1864, and is interred there in grave no. 9735.

When the war ended, Captain Henry Wirz, prison commandant, was tried and executed for war crimes, as he conspired to "impair and injure the health" of Union prisoners and commit "murder in violation of the laws of war." With a reputation for engaging in cruel and sadistic treatment of POWs, Wirz became the only person executed for war crimes during the Civil War. Melvin started a diary in 1861 when Company K was encamped near Washington. Initially, his daily account of soldiering focused on sightseeing, grand military reviews and an opportunity to shake hands with Lincoln. However, upon his arrival at Andersonville on June 3, 1864, the diary becomes an important documentation of the struggles of prison existence. As previously reported, the 1882 Concord Town Report affirmed the "inhumanity and torture" of the Union soldiers who arrived at Andersonville, and it's all detailed in Melvin's diary:

> *May 19th, 1864* [near Fredericksburg]
> *Struck our tents about noon, marched on quick time down the hill, then countermarched, lay on a hill, then went down and our battalion went after the Rebs. The fire was awful. I was taking Boardman to the rear. I had to leave him, and I saw the Rebs behind me. I surrendered. They did not fire, after. I got a horse to ride and the provost guard took me. I could not wish to be better treated. I slept rough, but was truly thankful for my treatment. Sold my coffee for Confederate scrip.*

On the day that Samuel Melvin was captured, Nathaniel Hawthorne died in his sleep while on a White Mountains tour with his friend, former president Franklin Pierce. Hawthorne's wife, Sophia, was too grief-stricken to orchestrate the funeral arrangements. Hawthorne's literary friends, perhaps including pallbearers Emerson and Bronson Alcott, in resistance to his widow's wishes, opened the casket during the service at Concord's First Parish Church. With Pierce in attendance, this created an appalling scene in which mourners casually viewed the remains, while family members turned away in horror.

Melvin's diary continues:

Friday, May 20th
Rather small rations, but the Rebs gave us good as they can. I will be glad when this cruel war is over, but it must be fought to the bitter end. Saw Gen'l Lee. We are treated with great kindness by our captors.

Saturday, May 21 and Sunday, May 22nd
No rations all day. Marched all day, started early, did not rest, nor have anything to eat. It was indeed truly painful. Got to a little brook, piled down on the ground for the night...such is the life of a prisoner in the hands of the Rebels, but while there is life there is hope. Here we are, Sunday morning and how good some beans would go...Turned in an old barn, got I pint of [corn]meal and 2 oz. of pork, all we had since Friday morning, and after marching 35 and riding 40 miles.

Monday, May 23rd
Rode on a platform car to Lynchburg—90 miles. It was tough, but we stood it. The most we had to eat was cinders from the engine. I shall be glad when we get to our journey's end, where we get something to eat.

Tuesday, May 24th
Got some rations. I ate quite hearty for a prisoner, and I felt like a new man altogether. I never knew what it was to be hungry before. I was so weak I could hardly stand. Oh how good a good meal would taste, such as I could get at home, but I must not dote on such things now.

Wednesday, May 25th
Don't I wish I could stop in some of our New England farmhouses and get a cup of milk? But never mind, I am looking forth with strong anticipations for our time of [prisoner] exchange; then it will be like a new Heaven for me and my comrades.

Thursday, May 26th
How strange a position we are in here. We are deprived of every solitary comfort of life, except thinking. That, no man can deprive us of. How glad [we will be] *when we are released.*

Friday, May 27th
Started about 6 o'clock from Lynchburg for Danville, packed in some box cars. It's about 150 miles and took us 24 hours. What a painful night we passed! No sleep, no place to lie down, nor scarcely to stand. No rations!

Sunday, May 29th
After riding all night and until 10 o'clock the next day, in a little box car, with 66 of us in it, with no sleep or chance to sleep, we got to Greensboro, N.C., a distance of 48 miles. Then, we got packed as thick as ever in a hog car, all manure. Where they will take us I do not know, but they say… "it's good enough for the Yank."

Monday, May 30th
How I wish I was in Boston with Dow, both free men! But never mind, we shall enjoy ourselves so much the better when we get home. I do think that we shall get exchanged by the 4th of July. If not, may the Powers help us.

Wednesday, June 1st
Started about 1 o'clock for Augusta [Georgia]; *met with an accident, two cars ran off the tracks. The men jumped off, and one of our men was killed, one had both legs broken, and many others were wounded.* [Then], *one of our men was shot through both feet by the accidental discharge of a musket. How sad to think of the poor fellows so far away from home and* [kin] *to be so suddenly killed or severely wounded.*

Thursday, June 2nd
We were almost starved when I got 6 good loaves of soft bread for a silver half. Gave one to each of us and it tasted good indeed. Then we ate our ration of corn cake, for it was growing stale fast. After getting all of that in us we felt once more something like ourselves.

This was the last good day before Melvin reached Andersonville prison. The remaining portions of the diary begin what was to become a four-month period during which there were 8,636 deaths at Andersonville, a 34 percent attrition rate in a camp in which there was an average of 25,241 prisoners.

Hell is empty...and all the devils are here...[Melvin quoted from Shakespeare's *The Tempest*]

Friday, June 3rd
Arrived at our camp...Andersonville, Georgia, where we were driven in next to the swamp. Capt. Wirz commands.

Saturday, June 4th
It is sad to see them carry the dead by into the dead house, a continual train of them all the time. How I hope that I shall live through it and be permitted to enjoy the true fruition of my life, which I have put so much confidence in and placed such bright anticipations upon! Still, if I die here I am sure that we shall die in a good cause, although in a brutal way.

Sunday, June 5th
Here we are in the same old pen...O'Lord! Hasten our release! Only think, if we were at the fort just one short month from today we should be honorably discharged...how I regret, how I sigh to think of our deplorable condition. Still, men have lived through rougher scenes than this, and if I take good care of myself, am very hopeful. But 'tis sad to see the dead go out, 100 per day. I have been a little ill, the beans gave me a very bad state of the stomach, but I think I shall be better tomorrow.

Monday, June 6th
The same as usual. Staid in our humble dwelling most of the time. It is such. It is life, and that is all.
  We managed to get a pint of rice for my 40 cents [prisoners bartering with what little money they had upon being captured].

Tuesday, June 7th
We are [hearing] *good reports from our Army, but can't believe any of them. There seem to be no signs for an exchange at all until the summer campaign is over, and I hope that will end with the downfall of Richmond.* [The downfall will not happen until ten months later.]
  My whole thoughts are on the joy we will have when we get in sight of our little starry banner. Oh how I would like to see it once more!

Saturday, June 11th
Had quite a rain and with our humble shelter it was no desirable thing. We got $3 worth of molasses in a quart cup and had some bread and molasses. Handy dealt it out by the spoonful…now we see what makes a thing good. Tongue nor pen can describe our privations here.

Sunday, June 12th
Great rumors in camp about our parole. Oh Lord, if they were only true…

Tuesday, June 14th
Another wet day for us. Handy had the shakes. Got our rations very late. One of [ours] *"passed to the summer land" last night. They are dying very fast. Corn meal gives me the diarrhea again.*

Wednesday, June 15th
1100 prisoners arrived…how sad are the reports from our regiment…53 from Company K killed, wounded and missing from the battle of the 19th [the day Melvin was taken prisoner].

Thursday, June 16th and Friday, June 17th
Did not see any from our regiment, but learned that ours had been badly cut up while charging the enemy's works on June 3rd. I feel for the Reg't and very specially for the old members. My stomach is not right yet. Did not eat anything but rice and had a severe day. Handy had his salt and spoon stolen. He has the shakes. Oh, I sigh for liberty.

My thoughts in the day and my dreams in the night are nothing but my liberty, my liberty.

Tuesday, June 21st
One man shot because he accidentally got over the dead-line [boundary line established by the guards; go beyond it, and you were shot].

Friday, June 24th
No joy or gladness is left. Perhaps too, I might refer to my soldier comrades who now lie buried in the cold ground, some even without a covering. How many, alas, have perished since 6 weeks next Sunday. Awful hot! Nothing of importance is going on, the same dull deplorable life. Diarrhea again. How good a word from friends would be.

Sunday, June 26th and Monday, June 27th
Got mush and meal, very good for this accursed land…if next month doesn't release us, Oh God, I would [wish] I had never been born.

Thursday, June 30th
Did not get anything but a little mush and meal for 2 days. It is rough, it is bad and to me it is almost unsupportable. How rough it is to serve our Country through so many privations for 3 long years, then, instead of going to that longed-for-home of joy and happiness, be put in this pen of insatiate misery. If anybody was ever miserable, I am since coming here.

Saturday, July 2nd
Here we are at this late day still living on corn meal and water…H, L and I have got a bad diarrhea again, making us feel quite blue.

Sunday, July 3rd
Only think, tomorrow is the immortal 4th. If I were only in Boston my joy would be unspeakable. My bowels are bad yet. The guard killed a crazy man for going over the dead-line. Had two roll calls and no rations at all.

Monday, July 4th
Not a sign of any celebration…no rations! One year ago today we had a good dinner and time in the tent at Fort Albany. Oh dear, I am discouraged.

Tuesday, July 5th
How long must we stay here? None but the functionaries in Washington can tell. I feel very badly with the headache and diarrhea. I went to see the doctor, but there was none.

Thursday, July 7th
I dreamed last night of being paroled…[what] disappointment when I awoke and found myself still in Hell.

Friday, July 8th
One year ago we were in first rate quarters in the tents at Albany, and we had as good [a] living as we cared about. The blackberries and sugar never gave out, and we used to eat about a quart apiece. Three times a week we had *plum-duff* [a plum pudding with currants and raisins]. My tent had a nice cool cellar and we had a large stone jar which we kept full

of butter. Then we had a pint of milk morning and evening in our coffee, making it like home.

Sunday, July 10th
Today, sad news indeed, I must record. I learned [from] Bridges that brother Asa was shot through the heart while charging the breastworks at Petersburg, June 16th. Bridges got to him just in [time] to stop some officers robbing his pockets. Bridges took his pocket-book containing $14.62, a few stamps and his bible and gave them to the chaplain. That is consoling.

Monday, July 11th
Today I saw six victims hung for murdering their fellow prisoners. They are the first ones I ever saw hung. How I want to get home….Now Asa is gone; if James has not survived, I am left alone. [James was the fourth brother to enlist and the only Melvin to survive the war.]

Thursday, July 14th and Friday, July 15th
Not so hot as usual, but things go bad. As for exchange or parole, I am about played out hoping for such a thing. The sergeants went to see the Captain [Wirz] and he told them he would shell us till not a man was left if any attempt was made to break out. Oh, God! Deliver us from this prison. I am not very well and never shall be while they keep me in here… [it] is not fair for us to be kept here. It is unjust, for the sake of humanity or Christianity, or anything that pretends to be civilized.

Sunday, July 17th
I am in a bad condition, nothing but water passes me and no appetite for anything…this corn meal is awful sickening. Oh, God! The man that will take me out of this I will call him Prince of Kings & Lord of Lords. He to me, will be a true redeemer.

Monday, July 25th
A fellow in Company G died at 8 this evening—through mere discouragement. That heartsickness, only known to young men like us, can never be imagined until it has been endured.

Wednesday, July 27th
A man [was] shot dead for stepping over the dead-line. I call that murder.

Wednesday, August 10th
Asa Rowe died this afternoon and was carried out and buried with the rest of the poor prisoners. I am sorry that he must so end his life, but it was ordered to be…

Sunday, August 14th
Things are very quiet. [In point of fact, the record indicates that trustees carried out 114 bodies on this day in 1864.]

Monday, August 15th
Today is the day for us to be paroled, but no signs of it yet and my faith is growing less.

Monday, September 12th
Today I have the saddest to record. Poor E.K. Holt's throat grew worse and he could not eat anything…he died about dusk, very hard indeed, choked to death. About an hour before he died he told me if he did not live till morning, to carry his bible to his father and tell him that he read it through once, the New Testament twice…and give his love to his sisters and mother.

Wednesday, September 14th
This morn I could hardly stand. Wilder carried my things for me, and by the help of a cane I got along a few rods. Got down to the depot and could not walk. Got an ambulance and took me to the hospital. It is an awful nasty, lousy place and I am disgusted. My diarrhea is very bad and will soon carry me off, if it is not checked, I am afraid.

Thursday, September 15th
Lay on my back all day. Eat not much; can't eat much; the corn bread I hate and the rice I can't, for it goes directly through me. I have seen no doctors yet. I am lying in a tent on a rubber blanket…the tent and blankets are just as full of lice and fleas as ever can be. As things look now, I stand a good chance to lay my bones in old Georgia, but I'd hate to as bad as one can, for I want to go home.

This is the last entry in the diary of Samuel Melvin. Two days after writing this, 130 prisoners died, and on September 25, Sam joined their ranks. He is buried at Andersonville, grave no. 9735.

Melvin purchased his diary book in Waltham in 1859 and began his war journal in 1861, continuing to maintain his daily log while at Andersonville. Following Sam's death, the diary came into the hands of a chaplain, who gave it to one of Melvin's comrades. It was then presented to the Melvin family and ultimately published in the Melvin Memorial dedication book.

Over the course of the war, 408,000 Civil War soldiers on both sides became POWs. More than 56,000 were to die under nightmarish conditions, with the mortality rate at Andersonville at 30 percent.

Referring to that part of Sleepy Hollow where rest Louisa May Alcott, Emerson, Thoreau, Hawthorne, Colonel George Prescott, Lieutenant Ezra Ripley and John Melvin, a James Russell Lowell poem ended with, "And here [are] great [people] who did great things."

Among the great Melvins, James was the last of the brothers to enlist and the only one of the four to return from the war. One of the youngest members of the Grand Army, he was a private in the 6th Massachusetts Volunteers, a unit that entered its third term of service on July 15, 1864, and mustered out on October 27. The 6th proceeded to Washington in July and was assigned to Arlington Heights, subsequently transferring to Fort Delaware on Pea Patch Island in Delaware Bay, where the regiment guarded a camp of seven thousand Confederate prisoners. In an odd twist of fate, James Melvin was guarding Confederates in Delaware while brother Sam was incarcerated by Rebels in Georgia.

Following his return to Concord at the end of October 1864, James Melvin became a prominent Boston businessman and was considered a principal figure in the development of the city's North End market district. Following the deaths of Asa, John and Samuel, James vowed that he would erect a memorial as a tribute to his fallen brothers. In 1897, he approached Concord sculptor and longtime friend Daniel Chester French to create the monument. French moved to Sudbury Road in Concord in 1867 and, twelve years later, built a studio next to the family home. His first notable work was the *Minute Man* statue commissioned by the Town of Concord and unveiled at the centenary of the Battles of Lexington and Concord on April 19, 1875, with President Grant presiding at the ceremony. Best known for the statue of Abraham Lincoln at the Lincoln Memorial (1920), Dan French's other sculptures include *John Harvard* in Harvard Yard and the bronze doors at the Boston Public Library, as well as his design of the Pulitzer Prize Gold Medal.

The Melvin Memorial, *Mourning Victory*, finished in 1908, consisted of an image of "Victory" with her eyes downcast while clutching the American flag. The tablet below the image is engraved as follows:

In memory of three brothers born in Concord
Who as soldiers, gave their lives in the war to save the country
This memorial is placed here by the surviving brother, himself a private
soldier in the same war.
I with uncovered head
Salute the sacred dead
Who went and return not.

The slate memorial was constructed in the Italian Renaissance style, with a twenty-eight-foot-high shaft and a platform measuring twenty-five by eight feet. The female figure "Victory," shrouded in the flag, is seven feet high, with three tablets below it, set side by side; each one is six by three feet.

On June 16, 1909, the forty-fifth anniversary of Asa's death, eighty-eight members of the 1st Massachusetts Heavy Artillery traveled to Concord from Boston in two special railroad cars to take part in Concord's Melvin Memorial dedication. Escorted in town by twenty members of Old Concord Post No. 180 of the Grand Army of the Republic, they were transported in horse-drawn barges to Old Concord Post, the armory on Walden Street (now known as "51 Walden," home to the Friends of the Performing Arts). Following a ceremony at the armory, presided over by two veterans of the 1st, Colonel J. Payson Bradley and Lieutenant Peter Smith, the assemblage marched to Sleepy Hollow for the dedication. Following singing by the Grand Army Glee Club, Lieutenant Smith opened the exercises with these words:

We are standing in this silent camping-ground of the dead, where many of our comrades who went with us in 1861 and 1865 are sleeping, resting, waiting for the roll-call above. It recalls to us, comrades and friends, those days when these three boys were young, the same as we…and they went out in Company K…and gave the best of their years to the service of our country…their battle has been fought, their victory won, and they are now waiting for those of us who tarry here a little longer, to come and join with them in the great parade above.

Next, the Glee Club sang "Tenting To-night on the Old Camp Ground," followed by an invocation of God's blessing on the three brothers who "showed their love for their imperiled country." Then the Glee Club provided a rousing rendition of Julia Ward Howe's "Battle Hymn of the Republic." Colonel Bradley was called on and delivered these unscripted remarks: "From the plough in the field, with only a few minutes warning,

The Melvin Memorial tomb, Sleepy Hollow. *Author's collection.*

without even going home to put on a different [garment], [Asa] went to the armory of your home company of the 5th Massachusetts Militia, enrolled himself in it and went to battle for his country. And as the war progressed, one after another of these boys entered the army, until, before the close of the war, the four brothers were serving under the stars and stripes."

At the conclusion of the dedication, the Old Concord Post escorted the 1ˢᵗ Massachusetts Heavy Artillery veterans to the Colonial Inn in the center of town, where formal photographs were taken. James Melvin hosted the entire group as his guests for an afternoon dinner in the main dining room of the inn. The menu featured a choice of four entrées, with "Concord asparagus," perhaps from Asparagus Farm on Bedford Street, and dessert that included strawberries from Concord. At the conclusion of dinner, James Melvin spoke to his guests:

> *I am deeply touched that so many of you are here.* [Lucien Wilder] *comes a thousand miles to pay a last tribute of love and affection to his friend and comrade, with whom he suffered at Andersonville. The face of this comrade was probably the last friendly one my brother ever saw. I also desire to express my gratitude to the Sleepy Hollow Cemetery Committee, for every member of that committee has done all in his power to cooperate with* [Dan French] *and myself. Also, I wish to thank the Concord Artillery for detailing a guard for this occasion. This old Concord Company is the one in which my brother served when it went to the front early in 1861.* [As] *for Andersonville, there can be no excuse. The barbarity and cruelty there will forever remain a blot on American civilization.*

Bradley then introduced Lucien Wilder to the audience, and in his remarks, Wilder spoke of Andersonville Prison, a subject he rarely mentioned:

> *As we entered the* [prison] *stockade, the old prisoners, who had been there* [upward of] *twelve months, were standing in line in rags, some of them almost nude—their hides the color of leather.* [They were] *living skeletons. No skeleton in a dime museum would ever compare with those men. They were simply skin and bones. After some five weeks I noticed that the men commenced to fail. There seemed to be no disease particularly, but a sort of despondency. A man would lie there and groan and look up at the sky and think of the old farm. He soon passed away.*

It was then that another comrade closed the Melvin Memorial with "the soldier's last tattoo":

> *For them the muffled drum has beat*
> *The soldier's last tattoo;*
> *No more on life's parade shall meet*

The 3rd Heavy Artillery Massachusetts, with two Concord soldiers in the ranks. *Author's collection.*

That brave and fallen few.
On Fame's eternal camping-ground
Their silent tents are spread,
And glory guards with solemn round
The bivouac of the dead.

Of those heroic dead who lie buried in Concord, none merit more praise than Asa, John, Samuel and James Melvin. They lie at rest.

Five days following Samuel Melvin's death at Andersonville, Captain Daniel Foster, former pastor at Concord's Trinitarian Church, was killed near Richmond at Chaffin's Farm, Virginia. Foster, an ardent abolitionist, enlisted on August 13, 1862, as a chaplain with the 33rd Massachusetts Volunteers and subsequently resigned to accept a captaincy with the 37th United States Colored Troops. An advocate of adopting a militant posture on the subject of slavery, Foster lived with his wife and child at the former house of H.D. Thoreau on Main Street. As a tribute to his service, as well as ten other parishioner-soldiers, including the Melvin brothers, a bronze plaque with their names inscribed was hung on the south wall of the sanctuary in the Trinitarian Congregational Church. Foster's regiment of black troops was charging over strong Confederate fortifications when he was killed in action.

A second regiment to be organized under President Lincoln's Bureau of U.S. Colored Troops, with Concord's Colonel John Ames serving as a regimental commander, was the 6th United States Colored Troops. This regiment was cited for heroism at New Market Heights in late September 1864. Several soldiers in this unit received the Medal of Honor, prompting Major General Benjamin Butler to issue a special order on October 11 that stated the following: "Of the colored soldiers, better men were never better led; better officers never led better men." Lincoln himself, writing in 1864 on the courageous actions of black troops, a majority of whom were from the South, wrote, "So far as tested, difficult to say they are not as good soldiers as any."

In addition to the 37th and the 6th, two other Concord soldiers served in additional colored regiments. George Buttrick, who was a corporal in the 5th in 1861, became a lieutenant colonel in the 75th United States Colored Troops, and George Willis, with prior service as a sergeant in the 1st Massachusetts Volunteers, rose to the rank of lieutenant in the 118th United States Colored Troops. The 118th participated in the siege against Petersburg and on April 3 was among the units occupying Richmond.

Toward the middle of July, in a desperate move intended to shock Northerners and split Grant's army near Richmond, Lee sent a larger portion of his troops to threaten Washington. On July 11, General Jubal Early and fifteen thousand Confederate troops reached the outskirts of the nation's capital, and a day later, they were within five miles of the White House. Fort Stevens, one of sixty-eight forts along the perimeter of Washington, became the epicenter of this battle, with the 20th Massachusetts and possibly twelve Concord soldiers among the defenders. President Lincoln, accompanied by his wife, Mary, and two cabinet members, traveled to the fort to view the action, resulting in a very close encounter with the enemy. Mounting the breastworks and placing himself within range of Early's sharpshooters, who were firing multiple volleys, legend has it that Captain Oliver Wendell Holmes Jr., with the 20th, shouted to the commander in chief, "Get down you fool." Upon returning to the Executive Mansion, Lincoln reportedly informed his secretary that he had been angrily warned to duck or get his head shot off. Early's attack was repulsed, becoming the only Civil War battle to take place within the perimeter of Washington. After the Confederate withdrawal, the 3rd Massachusetts Heavy Artillery, with two Concord soldiers in the ranks—Private Waldo Dunn and musician Michael Murray—garrisoned the fort.

Chapter 9

THE BLOODLETTING ENDS AND CONCORD PAYS TRIBUTE TO A MARTYRED PRESIDENT

Coming into the last year of the war, there were about 120 Concord soldiers serving in twenty-seven Massachusetts infantry, artillery and cavalry regiments. Among the hometown soldiers on the battlefield in 1865 was Charles Heywood Bartlett, who enlisted in Company G, 32nd Massachusetts Volunteer Infantry, and ascended in rank from corporal to sergeant and then officer status as second lieutenant in the 32nd. Born on Walden Street to a farming family, he later resided in a home on the easterly corner of Hubbard and Devens Streets. Participating in a Union offensive at Hatcher's Run during the Siege of Petersburg, Bartlett was wounded by a musket ball, which imbedded itself in his shoulder, thus terminating his active service as a soldier—he thereafter received a pension of eight dollars per a month. Rewarded for his service to the Union army, he was appointed paymaster for the U.S. Navy in 1869, a position he held until his death in 1872. In 1889, in a tribute before the Concord Antiquarian Society, Bartlett was credited with displaying a great fidelity to duty, an exceptional courage and "self-sacrificing patriotism…a life worth living."

Edward Jarvis Bartlett (1842–1914) enlisted as a private in F Company, 44th Massachusetts Volunteer Infantry, on August 19, 1862, and after service in North Carolina, he mustered out on June 18, 1863. He then served in a Nashville, Tennessee recruiting office, enlisting colored regiments, and on July 5 the following year, he was commissioned second lieutenant in the 5th Regiment, Massachusetts Volunteer Cavalry. Organized at Camp Meigs, Readville, the 5th was the first cavalry regiment from this state to be composed entirely of black troops. Following his military service, Bartlett was with the U.S. Sanitary Commission. On the 100th anniversary of Lincoln's birth, Bartlett recalled seeing the president in Richmond on April 3, 1865, and shared this memory with Concord Town Meeting members:

> *I wonder if there are any in this audience, except the veterans of the Civil War, who ever saw Abraham Lincoln. I saw him first in Washington, and also in Virginia, where he often came to see "his boys" as he was fond of calling the soldiers and many of them were little more than boys. But I want to tell you of the last time I saw him.*
>
> *On the morning of April 3, 1865, the City of Richmond, Virginia, was occupied by the Union troops and it was my good fortune to be a soldier in that army, serving as a lieutenant in the 5th Massachusetts Cavalry, then under the command of our* [Quincy] *neighbor, Colonel Charles Francis Adams* [great-grandson of President John Adams]. *When we reached the lower part of the city by the waterside, we saw a number of boats and steamers coming up the James River. One boat was at the wharf and its party had landed. Surrounding them was a great crowd, mostly darkies, who shouting and cheering were wild with excitement as the party, consisting of a squad of sailors escorting a number of officers and citizens, came up the street.*
>
> *In the center of the group I recognized President Lincoln. He wore a dark overcoat and a very high silk hat, which made him appear much taller than the officers beside him, in their low military caps. He led by the hand his young son Tad, then twelve years old, who walked beside him and had some trouble in keeping step with his father's long strides. As he approached I had just time to swing my company into line, and to give him the salute with raised saber, which he acknowledged by lifting his hat as he passed by.* [On April 3, Richmond fell, and on the night of April 14, Lincoln was shot.]
>
> *This is the last time I saw Abraham Lincoln. He was murdered ten days afterwards at Ford's Theater in Washington.*
>
> *He had finished his work. The great war was ended. The shackles were* [removed] *from the slaves.*

Edward Bartlett, known as "Ned" by family and friends, was the son of Dr. Josiah and Martha Tilden Bradford Bartlett. Initially, the family homestead was on Monument Street, but they relocated to 35 Lowell Road, where Dr. Bartlett had a medical practice and served the temperance cause, with strong antislavery leanings as well. Throughout his wartime years, Ned corresponded frequently with family members, assuring them that he was healthy and safe. Containers of his correspondence from 1860 to 1865, consisting of two dozen letters, are stored in the archives at the Concord Library.

In tribute to his service to the nation, an Edward Jarvis Bartlett tablet hangs from the west wall of the sanctuary in his place of worship, First Parish in Concord.

On April 19, four days after Lincoln's death, a town-wide memorial service for the fallen president was held at the First Parish Church, with Concord's Civil War veterans leading the processional. Mourners recognized this as a day that would reverberate, never to be forgotten. The communion table, covered in black cloth, was placed in front of the sanctuary, below the steps leading to the pulpit. A basket of white flowers and a wreath of English violets prepared by Edith Emerson was placed on top of the table. In front of the pulpit, shrouded in black, was a picture of Abraham Lincoln. The parish's minister, Reverend Grindall Reynolds, described the Lincoln assassination as "the blackest day in my memory, when we heard of the atrocious and meaningless murder of my great and good president."

In his remarks to mourners who filled Concord's church as the president's body was returning home by train to Springfield, Ralph Waldo Emerson captured the "quintessentially American" qualities of a president who rose from log cabin to the White House. Selections from his eloquent remarks appear here:

> *We meet under the gloom of calamity which darkens down over the minds of good* [people] *in civil society, as the fearful* [news] *travels over sea, over land, from country to country, like the shadow of an uncalculated eclipse over the planet. Old as history is, and manifold as are its tragedies, I doubt if any death has caused so much pain to mankind as this has caused, or will cause. In this country, on Saturday, everyone was struck dumb…as they meditated on the ghastly blow.*
>
> [Lincoln] *was the most active and hopeful of men, and his work has not perished; but acclamations of praise for the task he had accomplished burst out into a song of triumph, which even tears for his death cannot keep down.*
>
> *The president stood before us as a man of the people. He was thoroughly American—had never crossed the sea…a quite native, aboriginal man, as an acorn from the oak…Kentuckian born, working on a farm, a flatboatman, a captain in the Black Hawk War, a country lawyer, a*

representative in the rural legislature of Illinois-on such modest foundations the broad structure of his fame was laid. [Initially], *when the new and comparatively unknown name of Lincoln was announced, we heard the result coldly and sadly...it seemed too rash on a purely local reputation, to build so grave a trust in such anxious times...* [as it turned out] *we did not begin to know the riches of his worth.*

[While] *he offered no shining qualities at the first encounter, he did not offend by superiority. He had a face and manner which disarmed suspicion, which inspired confidence, which confirmed good-will. He was without vices and had a strong sense of duty.* [Lincoln] *was excellent in working out the sum for himself; in arguing his case and convincing you fairly and firmly. Then, he had a vast good nature, which made him tolerant and accessible to all; fair-minded, leaning to the claim of the petitioner... affable,* [with] *a good nature* [that revealed] *a noble humanity. His broad good humor, in which he delighted and in which he excelled, was a rich gift to this wise man. He was the author of a multitude of good sayings, so disguised as pleasantries...only later, by their acceptance and adoption,* [do these words] *turn out to be the wisdom of the hour. His brief speech at Gettysburg will not be easily surpassed by words on any recorded occasion.*

The man grew according to the need. His mind mastered the problem of the day; and as the problem grew, so did his comprehension of it. The new pilot was hurried to the helm in a tornado. Rarely was man so fitted to the event. He stood a heroic figure in the center of a heroic epoch.

Having been present at First Bull Run, Edwin Shepard Barrett recalled his "good fortune" to be in attendance at the Grand Review of the victorious Union army as it paraded along Pennsylvania Avenue right past the White House in May 1865. Speaking to the Concord audience in the town hall in 1886, he referenced the sea of flags that fluttered all along the avenue and the sixty-five thousand splendid veteran soldiers marching from the Capitol to the Treasury Building, displaying their battle-scarred regimental flags that "had waved over many a bloody field...In this brilliant array I saw the men from Concord, playmates at school, who for valiant services had risen from ranks to a high command. Men from Company G were there, who had received their baptism at Bull Run." It required a full six hours for this army, led by General Meade, to pass the reviewing stand, now occupied by the seventeenth president, Andrew Johnson. Barrett closed his remarks by indicating that the Grand Review was a fitting close to four years of war and

Daniel Chester French's Lincoln Memorial. *Author's collection.*

now the "vast armies of the North and South had fallen back into paths of peace, while half a million soldiers slept in their untimely graves."

One of the last Concord casualties of the war was Private Charles Nealy, a former member of the 1st Battalion Heavy Artillery, with prior service in the 5th Massachusetts Volunteers. Like Samuel Melvin before him, Nealy was a POW at Andersonville, and on June 14, at thirty-eight years, seven months and twenty-four days old, he died from the effects of his imprisonment. The 1865–66 Town Report reveals an expenditure of $24.50 for Healy's coffin, robe and cloth. Interred in Concord, his name is among the forty-eight engraved on the soldiers' monument in Monument Square.

At Harvard's Commemoration Day the following month, Emerson paid tribute to the 20th Massachusetts Volunteers, a regiment that included twenty-three Concord soldiers, five of whom died in the war (Thomas Mack, Edward Garrity, John McDonough, Charles Mohr and Charles Brigham). Eight of the officers in this unit, all casualties in the war, were Harvard College men. In his address, Emerson paid tribute to the character of these soldiers, some of whom were "scholars who changed the black coat for the blue…these peaceful, amiable men went out from the college to war…a war that gave back integrity to this erring and immoral nation."

It is said that young men fight wars started by old men and that some general comfortably situated in the rear echelon sends men into hostile fire to make some magnificent push without regard to cost. Indeed, General William Tecumseh Sherman, who marched against Atlanta and captured Savannah, bemoaned the reality of war in which one class of men makes war and leaves another to fight it out. Nonetheless, in recording his memories of Concord's young men in the Civil War, Reverend Grindall Reynolds applauded their devotion to country and strong desire to do all that was required, even suffer and die, in the interest of ensuring that the nation survived. On a larger scale, a Confederate memorial at Arlington National Cemetery beautifully captures the sacrifices on both sides of the war:

> *Not for fame or reward,*
> *Not for place or rank,*
> *Not lured by ambition or goaded by necessity,*
> *but in simple obedience to duty as they understood it—*
> *They suffered all, sacrificed all, dared all, and died.*

The only debt we can never repay is the debt we owe to our courageous defenders.

The cost of four years of war was excessive. Northern losses were close to 650,000 dead, wounded and missing, with Southern casualties estimated at 475,000. That's an attrition rate of 10 percent for the Union army and 25 percent for the Confederacy. The most significant numerical loss from a single engagement was the Battle of Gettysburg, where more than 40,000 Americans were killed or wounded. National Park Service figures stipulate that Massachusetts provided 122,781 white troops, 2,996 African American troops and 19,983 sailors, for a total of 146,730. From this number, there were 13,942 casualties from the commonwealth, with this statistical breakdown:

- 6,115 killed
- 5,530 died from disease or sickness
- 257 were listed as accidental deaths
- 557 died from "causes except battle"
- 1,483 died as POWs

Of the 450 enrolled Concord soldiers and sailors, 48 became Civil War fatalities, with 21 battlefield deaths and 27 identified as casualties dying from disease or sickness related to their service to the Union. The causes and numbers of non-combat Concord deaths include the following:

- typhoid (6 soldiers)
- malarial fever (3)
- disease (3)
- consumption (2)
- sunstroke (2)
- chills (1)
- fever (1)
- chronic dysentery (1)
- gangrene (1)
- cholera (1)
- erysipelas (1), an acute fever resulting from tissue inflammation
- pneumonia (1)
- "died in service" (1)
- "in hospital" (1)
- "lingering sickness" (2, Sam Melvin and Charles Nealy, due to time at Andersonville)

Beyond the forty-eight fatalities, an indeterminate number of our Concord Civil War battlefield soldiers received wounds from which they later recovered.

Upon visiting nameless graves at the soldiers' cemetery near his cool summer cottage at the Soldier's Home, Lincoln uttered this memorable tribute to the self-sacrificing dead:

> *...and women over the graves shall weep,*
> *where nameless heroes calmly sleep.*

In compiling the 1865–66 Town Report, Concord selectmen summarized the last year of the war thusly: "Through the great Civil War, the manhood, the wealth and the spirit of Concord were poured out for the Union and to put down the rebellion."

In their report to townspeople, the School Committee, chaired by Grindall Reynolds, with Emerson in the ranks, issued this preface to the summary of the 1865–66 school year: "While we were in the midst of a great Civil War, when all our energies and resources were taxed to the utmost, when every eye and heart were turned towards those battlefields where our friends were incurring every hardship and daring every peril, and where the fate of the nation was being decided…we can be thankful…that we have passed through the agonies and throes of a great rebellion."

On the fiscal side, the 1865–66 report listed the following war-related expenditures:

- *$1000 remaining unpaid of the war debt* [which was initially contracted in 1862].
- *$21.50 for printing of warrants and order of services at the funeral services of Abraham Lincoln* [First Parish Church on April 19].
- *$210.98 in expenses for firing salutes on the taking of Richmond and the surrender of Lee's Army in April, along with firing "minute" guns during the funeral ceremonies of President Lincoln.*

Looking toward 1866–67, there would be a request to raise $1,000 toward the creation of the soldiers' monument in the center of Concord. This initial expense would cover the designer's fee, surveyor's cost, a fence, lumber and $500 for two inscription plates.

Chapter 10

POSTWAR CONCORD

"Faithful Unto Death"

T he lure of the Civil War has remained strong for 150 years, and the soldiers who fought in that war established a strong fraternity, one that may have been best expressed by "Private Miles O'Reilly," a pseudonym for a New York poet by the name of Charles Halpine:

> *There are bonds of all sorts in this world of ours...*
> *The girl and the boy are bound by a kiss,*
> *But there's never a bond, old friend, like this,*
> *We have drank from the same canteen.*

The obelisk in Monument Square, tapering and rising in a pyramid, was erected on April 19, 1867, and bears the bronze tablet names of forty-eight departed heroes "who found in Concord a birthplace, home or grave." The motto "Faithful Unto Death" is etched on one side of the monument, with the dates of the war on the other side. Nearby was an elm tree under which Reverend William Emerson rallied the town on the morning of the 1775 fight; on this day, ninety-two years later, his descendant, Ralph Waldo Emerson, delivered an address in the shade of the same tree. Recalling the minutemen of 1775, Emerson stirred his fellow townspeople with these lines:

> *We come to consecrate this stone to heroes of to-day,*
> *Who perished in a holy cause as gallantly as they.*
> *As on their former muster fields called by its notes again,*

Left: Sergeant Edward Hosmer's grave. He died in Baton Rouge, Louisiana. *Author's collection.*

Right: George Algeo's grave, 1st Battalion, Massachusetts Volunteers. *Author's collection.*

Those ancient heroes seem to greet brave Prescott and his men.
And as each soldier saint appears to answer to his name,
Not one has dimmed the luster of its old unconquered fame.

In Emerson's view, now that the country was reunited and freed from the stain of slavery, this soldiers' monument would forever stand.

Five years later, the town began to lay plans for the 1875 centennial of the Battle at the Old North Bridge, a suspension that spans the Concord River, close to the confluence of the Assabet and Sudbury Rivers at Egg Rock. In March 1873, there was an affirmative town meeting vote to "procure a statue of a Continental Minute-Man, cut in granite, and erect it on a proper foundation on the American side of the river." It was also determined that Daniel Chester French, a twenty-five-year-old Concord sculptor, would be commissioned to design the bronze statue of the minuteman to be dedicated on April 19, 1875. In November 1873, French submitted for the committee's review a small plaster model of what was to become a figure described by George Bartlett as "the Minute-Man of the day, with wonderful truth and vigor of action." John Shepard Keyes, Lincoln's bodyguard and a U.S. marshal, chaired the Monument Committee, and Major General Francis Barlow served as chief marshal of the processional on celebration day. In the presence of President Grant, Vice President Henry Wilson and other dignitaries, the 5th Massachusetts Regiment and its Concord Artillery led the grand parade, accompanied by Washington's Marine Band, which had been ordered to Concord for the occasion.

Judge Ebenezer Hoar, former attorney general in the Grant administration and member of the U.S. Congress to follow, was to be "President of the Day" and, in that capacity, scripted every aspect of the celebration. In a letter to a family member, Louisa May Alcott described the decorative details of the celebration: "Judge Hoar wishes each man to decorate his mansion and get out his relics, and receive Grant with bursts of applause. Especially those who dwell in Revolutionary ruins, are ordered to scuttle the dust of ages, the ancestral rats, and venerable bugs out of sight and put their best foot forward."[19]

Inheriting her mother's activism, Louisa May was a strong supporter of women's suffrage, known to walk door to door for suffrage and feminist causes. Her mother, Abigail May Alcott, was an enthusiastic promoter of women's rights in marriage and the workforce, causes that were linked to the antislavery movement before the Civil War. These powerful connections between the abolitionist movement and women's rights embraced their common work from the time of the Seneca Falls Convention in New York (1848) and the beginning of the war in 1861. In the interest of pursuing the war effort, the movement was placed on hold during the war but was reignited following Lee's surrender at Appomattox. Women's involvement in the abolitionist cause and soldier's aid societies had provided women with a platform to organize, write, raise money and speak on behalf of slaves and soldiers. There was no turning back now. In 1880, Louisa May and nineteen other women broke a gender barrier by attending the Concord Town Meeting, and she became the first Concord woman to vote in a town election, casting a School Committee ballot. In a March 30, 1880 article submitted to the *Woman's Journal*, she reported that "[n]o bolt fell on our audacious heads...no earthquake shook the town."

On September 12, 1885, Concordians celebrated the town's 250th anniversary, with the Concord Artillery and the Old Concord Post, GAR, leading the parade. Richard Barrett was appointed chief marshal, an honor directly attributable to his distinguished wartime service as captain of Company G in the 47th Massachusetts Volunteer Militia, which was the second iteration of the Concord Artillery. Barrett and military units assembled in Monument Square at 9:30 a.m. and marched down Lexington Road to Heywood, Walden, Hubbard, Devens, Sudbury and Thoreau and to the top of Main Street and then were escorted to the Town House for 11:00 a.m. ceremonies. An elegant lunch was held off Main Street before South Bridge, behind the railroad tracks.

Two years later, at the March 1887 town meeting, townspeople voted an appropriation of $6,500 to cover the acquisition of a small plot of land situated between Walden Street and the Mill Brook, contiguous to the First Parish Church, to fund the construction of a building that would prove more suitable to store the 1846 Concord Artillery's brass cannons. This land at 51 Walden became the home of the Concord Armory from 1887 until damaged by a fire in 1912; it featured proximity to four acres of land gifted to the town in 1887 by heirs of Ralph Waldo Emerson and named the Emerson Playground. Designated ceremonial and recreation space, Emerson Playground also served as a military drill field and parade ground for the Concord Artillery. Later on, rooms were set aside for the Old Concord Post No. 180 of the GAR to conduct its meetings and host reunions. With construction of a new armory on Everett Street, the old armory was renamed the Veteran's Building in 1920 and, with the construction of a theatrical stage, became home to the Concord Players.

Having been the first from Concord to go to war, the 5th Massachusetts Volunteer Militia, with the Concord Artillery Company in the ranks, held a 5th Massachusetts Infantry Association Reunion in Concord on June 9, 1897. The theme was "Rally Round the Flag Boys, Rally Once Again." With eighty-three men on the Concord roster upon arrival in Washington in April 1861, this ninety-day unit engaged the enemy at First Bull Run; mustered out on July 31, 1861, and was then reinstated on September 16, 1862. The invitation began with this message:

> *As we grow older, let us cling together as our numbers diminish, pledge to each other new memories and an undying affection for the old flag.*
> *At dinner our stomachs well filled, good cheer will surely follow. We shall see lots of OLD things, and make ourselves YOUNG for the time at any rate.*
> *The Woburn band is engaged for the day.*
> *And we expect some of our old war songs from our comrades.*

The 5th Massachusetts Reunion invitation concluded with the posting of train fare from Boston to Concord and return, which was fifty-five cents, and a two-dollar program fee, dinner included.

On February 12, 1909, the 100th anniversary of the birth of Abraham Lincoln, a celebration of his life took place in Concord's town hall, with a public assembly scheduled at 3:30 p.m. Edward Bartlett, former second lieutenant in the 5th Massachusetts Cavalry, was appointed to the three-member committee that planned patriotic songs, recitations, speeches and personal reminiscences of Lincoln. John Shepard Keyes, having served as a delegate to the Republican Convention in 1860 and then Lincoln's bodyguard, was asked to relate his experiences with the late president. However, his advanced age and declining health prevented him from appearing. Instead, Edward Bartlett recalled his encounter with the martyred president during the occupation of Richmond in April 1865. As town residents were filling the hall, the Concord Artillery joined the veterans of Old Concord Post, GAR, in dress uniform and were then provided a place of honor in the hall.

After the assembly was called to order, the audience rose and joined the High School Chorus in singing "Marching Along," William Bradbury's patriotic war tune of 1861, with these select verses:

The army is gathering from near and from far,
The trumpet is sounding the call for the war;
A cheer for our leader, he's gallant and strong;
For God and our Country we're marching along.
The foe is before us in battle array,
But let us not waver, or turn from the way.
The Lord is our strength and the Union our song;
With courage and faith we are marching along.

Chairman Edward Emerson, Waldo's son, provided some brief remarks, identifying Lincoln's special qualities of courage in times of crisis, with a determination to simply present the "moral issue" and stay the course. Looking at the high school boys in attendance, Emerson reminded the audience that Lincoln's soldiers, strong and brave, were themselves just boys, most under twenty-one years old. John Garvey, of the high school, then proceeded to recite "Lincoln's address at the consecration of the National Cemetery at Gettysburg" (forty-six years later, not yet referred to simply as the "Gettysburg Address").

At the closing of Lincoln's 100th anniversary celebration, the audience sang Mrs. Julia Ward Howe's "Battle Hymn of the Republic." Her great-great-grandson, John Shaw, grew up in Concord, always hearing the "Battle Hymn" at celebrations, weddings and funerals. Eight months following the Lincoln program, Julia Ward Howe and a small group of abolitionists gathered in a brick house on Elm Street, the last house on the right before the bridge, to commemorate the 50th anniversary of John Brown's October raid at Harper's Ferry. Their host, another member of the "Secret Six" supporting Brown, was Franklin Sanborn, Concord's longtime schoolmaster and strident abolitionist. In addition to her antislavery struggle, Julia was a suffrage activist, forming the Massachusetts Suffrage Association with Lucy Stone among others. Julia's 1909 meeting at Sanborn's home followed a series of visits to this town, including a trip to Bronson Alcott's School of Philosophy in 1879, where she delivered a lecture titled "Modern Society." If, in her "Hymn," "God sounded forth the trumpet that shall never call retreat," Julia aroused the conscience of the nation with her own trumpet.

While declining in numbers, the remaining Concord Civil War veterans gathered for two celebratory events in the 1920s; these may have been their final muster calls. On April 19, 1925, Concord celebrated the 150th anniversary of the Battle of 1775, a day that was described as horribly cold, with a wet snowfall having occurred the night before. Conditions were so wet that a horse fell during the parade, and the rider sustained a broken leg. Among the committee members planning the celebration was George F. Wheeler, a Civil War veteran who had served with the 47th Massachusetts Volunteer Militia, a second-service Concord Artillery regiment, in action from September 1862 to September 1863. In 1928, the Concord Art Association provided a gift to the town, *Memories of Antietam*, which was gratefully accepted by town meeting vote the following year. This painting, by artist Elizabeth Wentworth Roberts (1871–1927), founder of the Concord Art Association, depicted sixteen Civil War veterans reviewing a painting of the Battle of Antietam. While none of these sixteen Concord veterans actually participated in the bloodiest single day of the war in September 1862, we recall John McDonough, a former Concord laborer who was killed at Antietam and is interred in the garden of heroes at Antietam National Cemetery. *Memories of Antietam* recently underwent extensive restoration at the Williamstown Art Conservation Center and was returned to the Town House in March 2013.

John McDonough was among those who fought, bled and died endeavoring to make the nation right. Massachusetts provided close to 6 percent of the total Union soldiers, with 75 percent of enlisted men, including McDonough, either farmers or laborers when they signed up. Concord enrolled 450 wartime volunteers, 48 of whom paid the ultimate price. We pay tribute to those who died "for cause and comrades."

The 1ˢᵗ Massachusetts Cavalry, with nine Concord soldiers in the ranks. *Author's collection.*

Concord Soldiers Who Died for Their Country in the "War of the Rebellion"

32ⁿᵈ **Massachusetts**: Colonel George L. Prescott, Sergeant Charles Appleton, Corporal William Damon, Private James Thompson, Private Francis Buttrick, Private Barney Clark, Private George Erskine and Private Jonas Melvin

2nd Massachusetts Volunteers: Private Thomas Carey

9th Massachusetts Volunteers: Captain James McCafferty Jr. and Private Martin Lynch

12th Massachusetts Volunteers: Private Paul Kittredge

16th Massachusetts Volunteers: Private Herman Flint

20th Massachusetts Volunteers: Private Charles Brigham, Private Edward Garrity and Private John McDonough

24th Massachusetts Volunteers: Private Charles Lawrence

26th Massachusetts Volunteers: Private James Billings, Private Thomas McGuire and Private Charles Brown

29th Massachusetts Volunteers: Lieutenant Ezra Ripley

38th Massachusetts Volunteers: Private Bertrand Burgess and Private Edwin Proctor

40th Massachusetts Volunteers: Private George Carr, Private Charles Hannaford and Private Alonzo Monroe

47th Massachusetts Volunteer Militia: First Sergeant Franklin Gregory, Corporal Erastus Kingsbury and Private Oliver Richards

53rd Massachusetts Volunteer Militia: Private Charles Stuart

56th Massachusetts Volunteers: Private Michael Murray

59th Massachusetts Volunteers: Private Richard Clark, Private George Poland and Sergeant Henry Smith

1st Massachusetts Heavy Artillery: Private Paul Dudley, Private Asa Melvin, Private John Melvin, Private Samuel Melvin and Private Charles Nealy

1st Massachusetts Cavalry: Private Thomas Doyle

4th Massachusetts Cavalry: Private Frederick Tarbell

7th Maine Volunteers: First Sergeant James Fernald

1st Michigan Volunteers: Private Alden Buttrick

11th Ohio Volunteers: Private Charles Wright

U.S. Hospital Service: Chaplain James Means and Chaplain William Whitcomb

37th U.S. Colored Troops: Captain Daniel Foster

U.S. Regular Army: Major General Amiel Whipple

To every man upon this earth
Death cometh soon or late.
And how can man die better
Than facing fearful odds,
For the ashes of his fathers,
And the temple of the Gods.
—*from Macaulay's* Lays of Ancient Rome

Notes

Introduction

1. Lockwood and Lockwood, *Siege of Washington*, 41.
2. Drawn from the title of McPherson's book, *For Cause and Comrades: Why Men Fought in the Civil War*.
3. Ibid., 22.

Chapter 1

4. Petrulionis, *To Set This World Right*, 113.

Chapter 2

5. Goodheart, *1861*, 41.
6. Holzer, *Lincoln*, 37.
7. Ibid., 51.

Chapter 3

8. O'Connor, *Civil War Boston*, 50.

Chapter 4

9. Schouler, *Massachusetts in the Civil War*, 134.

10. Lockwood and Lockwood, *Siege of Washington*, 199.
11. Schouler, *Massachusetts in the Civil War*, 154.
12. Guelzo, *Gettysburg*, 9.

Chapter 5

13. Shaara, *Blaze of Glory*, introduction.
14. From *Memoirs of Members of the Social Circle*, 2nd series.

Chapter 6

15. Sauers, *Civil War Chronicle*, 184.

Chapter 7

16. Atkinson, *Guns at Last Light*, 71.
17. Drawn from John S. Keyes's *Autobiography*.
18. Higginson, ed., *Harvard Memorial Biography*, 107.

Chapter 10

19. Quoted in the *Concord Journal*, March 28, 2011.

Bibliography

Books, Manuscripts and Collections

Adams, Charles. *Charles Francis Adams.* Boston: Houghton Mifflin, 1916.

Alcott, Louisa May. "Hospital Sketches and Campfire Stories." *Boston Commonwealth* magazine (1909). Dover Publications.

Atkinson, Rick. *The Guns at Last Light.* New York: Henry Holt and Company, 2013.

Barrett, Edwin S. *What I Saw at Bull Run.* Boston: Beacon Press, 1886.

Bartlett Family Papers. Concord Free Public Library, Concord, MA.

Bartlett, George. *Concord—Historic, Literary and Picturesque.* Boston: D. Lothrop Company, 1885.

Barton, William E. *Lincoln at Gettysburg.* Indianapolis, IN: Bobbs Merrill, 1930.

Billings, John D. *Hard Tack and Coffee.* Old Saybrook, CT: Konecky and Konecky, 1887.

Burchard, Peter. *Glory: One Gallant Rush.* New York: St. Martin's Press, 1965.

Detzer, David. *Donneybrook: The Battle of Bull Run.* New York: Harcourt Books, 2004.

Emerson, Jason. *Giant in the Shadows: The Life of Robert T. Lincoln.* Carbondale: Southern Illinois University Press, 2012.

Golay, Michael. *A Ruined Land: The End of the Civil War.* New York: John Wiley and Sons, 1999.

Goodheart, Adam. *1861: The Civil War Awakening.* New York: Alfred A. Knopf, 2011.

Guelzo, Allen C. *Gettysburg: The Last Invasion.* New York: Alfred A. Knopf, 2013.

Halberstadt, Hans. *The Soldiers Story: The American Civil War.* Washington, D.C.: Brassey's Inc., 2007.

Higginson, Thomas, ed. *Harvard Memorial Biography.* Bedford, MA: Applewood Books, 1867.

Holzer, Harold. *Lincoln: President-Elect.* New York, Simon and Schuster, 2008.

Holzer, Harold, ed. *The Lincoln Anthology.* New York: Library of New York, 1989.

————. *Lincoln as I Knew Him.* Chapel Hill, NC: Algonquin Books, 1999.

Howe, Florence H. *The Story of the Battle Hymn of the Republic.* New York: Harper and Brothers, 1916.

Keyes, John S. *Autobiography.* Owned and transcribed by the Concord Free Public Library, Concord, MA.

Lanier, Robert S. *The Photographic History of the Civil War.* New York: Review of Reviews Company, 1911.

Leech, Margaret. *Reveille in Washington.* New York: Harper and Brothers, 1941.

Lockwood, John, and Charles Lockwood. *The Siege of Washington.* New York: Oxford University Press, 2011.

Lowenfels, Walter. *Walt Whitman's Civil War.* New York: De Capo Press, 1960.

McPherson, James M. *For Cause and Comrades: Why Men Fought in the Civil War.* New York: Oxford University Press, 1997.

————. *This Mighty Scourge: Perspectives on the Civil War.* New York: Oxford University Press, 2007.

Melvin, James. *A Brother's Tribute.* Cambridge, MA: Riverside Press, 1909.

Melvin, Samuel. *Andersonville Diary.* 1864. Cambridge, MA: A.E. Roe, 1909.

Memoirs of Members of the Social Circle. Concord, MA: Riverside Press, 1888.

"Memories of Concord Veterans of the Civil War, 1861–1865." Vols. 1 and 2. Unpublished material, bound by Concord Free Public Library, circa 1890s.

Miller, Richard F. *Harvard's Civil War: A History of the 20th Massachusetts Volunteer Infantry.* Hanover, NH: University Press of New England, 2005.

O'Connor, Thomas H. *Civil War Boston.* Boston: Northeastern University Press, 1997.

Petrulionis, Sandra Herbert. *To Set This World Right: The Antislavery Movement in Concord.* Ithaca, NY: Cornell University Press, 2006.

Records of the Old Concord Post No. 180 of the G.A.R. Massachusetts Department, 1884–1890.

Reports of the Selectmen and Other Officers of the Town of Concord, 1860–1862. Concord Free Public Library.

Robertson, James I., Jr. *Soldiers Blue and Gray.* Columbia: University of South Carolina Press, 1998.

Sauers, Richard A. *Civil War Chronicle: 150th Anniversary.* Lincolnwood, IL: Legacy Publishing, 2011.

Schouler, William. *Massachusetts in the Civil War.* Boston: E.P. Dutton and Company, 1868.

Shaara, Jeff. *A Blaze of Glory: A Novel of the Battle of Shiloh.* New York: Ballantine Books, 2013.

Sheldon, George. *When the Smoke Cleared at Gettysburg.* Nashville, TN: Cumberland House Publishing, 2003.

Soldiers and Sailors of Concord, Massachusetts, 1861–1865. Report by the Committee Appointed by the Town. Concord, MA, 1908. Author's collection.

Stanhower, Daniel. *The Hour of Peril.* New York: St Martin's Press, 2013.

Titone, Nora. *My Thoughts Be Bloody.* New York: Free Press, 2010.

Town of Concord. *The Celebration in Concord of the 100th Anniversary of the Birth of Abraham Lincoln*, February 12, 1909. Concord, MA: self-published, April 6, 1909.

Wheeler, Ruth R. *Concord: Climate for Freedom.* Concord, MA: Concord Antiquarian Society, 1967.

NEWSPAPERS

Concord (MA) Journal. March 28, 2011.

Staunton (VA) Spectator. June 30, 1863, and January 22, 1864.

INDEX

About the Author

A retired university professor, Rick Frese now teaches part-time as an associate professor of sociology at Bentley University in Waltham, Massachusetts. A recipient of the university's prestigious President's Award for Excellence in Teaching, he has taught American and international politics in the Global Studies Department. A veteran of the U.S. Army, he and his wife, Nancy, are longtime residents of Concord, his mother's hometown.

Visit us at
www.historypress.net
....

This title is also available as an e-book